THE

DAYS OF WONDER

by G.W. Hardin

THE DAYS OF WONDER

Dawn of a Great Tomorrow

by G.W. Hardin

DreamSpeaker Creations, Inc.
Missoula, Montana • 2003

This is a true story. Some names have been changed at the request of the individual. Some scenes have been combined into a single scene for the purpose of bettering the story line.

First printing: February 2003

Publication Data
>   Hardin, G.W.
>   The Days of Wonder:
>   Dawn of a Great Tomorrow
>   Inspiration, Spirituality, New Age
>   pp. 240

>   ISBN 1-893641-01-5
>   1. Inspiration 2. Spirituality 3. New Age

Cover design: Ken Elliott, G.W. Hardin, and Gary LaCroix
Book design: G.W. Hardin

Set in 11 point Palatino typeface
Printed in the United States of America
Central Plains Book Manufacturing
      Arkansas City, KS

DEDICATION

Dedicated to all the "ordinary" people
who turn out to be so extraordinary

ACKNOWLEDGMENTS

To those who made this all possible in big and little ways, especially Nick Bunick, Beth Ayers, Julia Ingram, Brian Hilliard, Janet Hardin, Ken Elliott, Gary LaCroix, and Martha Granda Benet.

CONTENTS

THE
DAYS OF WONDER

fOREWORD

Hold onto your hats folks. You are about to have a wild adventure in reading! This book leads where few have traveled before! You are now entering the magical world that many believe in as children, but few do as adults. *The Days of Wonder* is not an ordinary book. It has the power to change your life!

From the very first chapter, strap on your roller blades as this riveting story unfolds at a pace almost more rapid than you can read. *The Days of Wonder* makes you wish you had taken Evelyn Woods reading courses so you would possess the skills to read faster and discover what is unfolding on the next page sooner.

This book is wonder-filled ... most sequels to books are a case of "instant disappointment," but *The Days of Wonder*, following on the heals of *The Messengers*, is powerful; it holds you spellbound! Reading the story holds you in a dichotomy: At one moment you want to read it slowly like wrapping your tongue around your favorite ice cream cone ... to savor every morsel of new knowledge and have it permeate your memory cells of enjoyment. And in the next moment you are the greedy sibling trying to bite off the biggest piece and chomp your way through the book. This sequel has a heart ... that beats with each written word.

When I read something spiritually uplifting, it is my habit to pencil little hearts in the margins, where the phrases/words of wisdom touch my heart. Soon after beginning to read the manuscript for this book, the pages resembled artwork rather than a piece of literature ... little hearts danced *everywhere* across the pages.

Do you ever wonder why Disneyland has the power over millions of people around the world, and why Disney's movies are viewed over and over by children, then again as adults? What is the magic of Harry Potter that addicts its readers to the series of books? It is belief. We all hold an inner belief in the power of good, angels, God ... and because we cannot see angels, God, magic or mystery as we age, our dreams of the Land of Oz fades from memory.

The Days of Wonder rekindles the small ember of trust in the mysteries of the Divine within you. This tiny ember will grow and flash into a full-blown blaze with each page you read. Maybe one of the most amazing things about Hardin's work is that the people in the book are real. Their life experiences are real. No one made this story up. If they had, the narration certainly would be one of the best fictional stories you have read in a long time. But the events in this story are not created from the blank slate of the author's mind ... they are true!

I personally know many of the people, you are about to meet, in this fascinating book, and watched over the years as their lives unfolded with the guidance of the Divine. Miracles appear around every corner to show us how smoothly things flow when we walk our true life's journey. The more the participants of this book focused their attention onto their life missions the clearer their path became and more miracles amazingly manifested.

What was God's original intention 2,000 years ago, what was She/He trying to demonstrate through Jesus and his disciples? Hopefully this book will rekindle a long hidden reminder in your heart and soul. It is now time for humanity to receive the full benefit of that message.

We have entered the days of wonder where the healers of our world are coming forward to teach various ways to end suffering. Obviously, this includes the assistance of the angelic realm. The angels can only help if we ask them, if we fully become ourselves.

The Days of Wonder teaches that the time of modern gurus and teachers is over. We are our own guru, our own teacher, our own healer. It offers methods you can employ in your own lives and those of your loved ones. Thus, this book moves from the leadership of Nick Bunick into the ways everyday people are coming forward to show us what it is we can do to bring healing to ourselves and our planet.

Modern day mystics reveal a new world and a new outlook to inspire us to embrace the future. Enjoy this amazing reading adventure into the lives of others and yourself!

On December 4th, 2002, I telephoned psychic Donna Seebos' radio show on KLAY 1480 AM, in Lakewood, Washington, and she said I would be receiving "a very important phone call on December 15th that would lead to wondrous things. I really like where this will be going," said Donna as if she was watching a great adventure into the future.

My first thought was that possibly a TV show would be picking up some stories from my second book, *A Christmas Filled with Miracles*, for the holiday season. A few weeks later, when I was traveling to Canada to visit my mother, I stopped for several days in Seattle to stay with Atira. Nothing monumental happened on the 15th. No one phoned me, but Atira had a few phone calls and one was from G.W. Hardin, co-author of the best-selling book *The Messengers*. The three of us have been friends for years and I thought nothing or extra-special had transpired ... other than to yell across the room, "HELLO."

While Atira was chatting with G.W. she said, "Hey, G.W. wants to know if you will write the foreword to his book *The Days of Wonder*." It is an honor to be asked and I quickly responded "Yes" and thought nothing more about it until the manuscript arrived three weeks later, and I started to read it. Only then did the realization strike, like a hard cold snowball, that the prophesy of Donna Seebo had come true ... this book is the fabulous news ... for all of us!

Mary Ellen "Angel Scribe"
Author, *Expect Miracles* and *A Christmas Filled with Miracles*
Editor, "Angels and Miracles Good-News-Letter"
P.O. Box 1004
Cottage Grove - OR 97424
MaryEllen@AngelScribe.com
www.AngelScribe.com

PART 1

OPENING THE JOURNAL

The Soft People

*I*t is here. Fanfares of trumpets did not announce its arrival, nor did marching bands welcome it, but it is here. The earth did not shake, nor did floodlights of the media brighten its coming. The Age of Wonders did not fly in on the wings of technological marvel, nor did it shatter the skies like the first atomic blast. But it is here. Grasp my hand while I escort you through the gateway to the Age of Wonders.

Perhaps, this great age floated in on the wing of a butterfly. No, even that would have been too obvious. The magnificent truth of it all is that it arrived held in the heart of a single child. That is how all great ages begin.

Nick leaned forward in his chair rereading a letter which held him spellbound. An admiring parent had written him. His left hand seemed to feel the power of its simple words while his other hand highlighted passages with a colored pencil. Nick's business world operated by these colored pencils. Important meetings, high-priority discussions, teleconferences spanning continents and great seas were color-coded in his executive diary by these pencils. But what fixed his eyes at this moment was far more important than anything his colored pencils had ever highlighted before. For at this moment his pencils highlighted evidence of the Age of Wonders. *Yes, it is here*, his red pencil whispered back and forth across the lettering, *it is here*.

May 4, 1997

Dear Mr. Bunick:

Since the publishing of *The Messengers*, I imagine that you have received a lot of letters like mine. Do with it what you will, I just felt the necessity to make contact with you about a couple of things.

My wife, Carolyn, bought the book, and we read it together over the period of a couple of weeks. We have personal knowledge of a story that confirms to us angelic presence. Daniel Meyers is 3 1/2 years old, and was born with a very serious congenital heart ailment. He has gone thorough several surgeries, and will experience more before he's through. His mother, Susan, offered the following testimony in worship at our church on April 6:

> This came from a series of quiet discussions with Daniel. It was one of those things that just flowed from me to the paper without thought. Later, when I read it, I felt lots of things, which I'm sure you will, too, but mostly I felt it should be shared.
>
> A child was born who was very ill. The doctors said he had very little chance of survival. His family felt the child was special. They prayed, they stayed by his side. The doctor saw the family's hope and felt the gift of this special child. Even in the darkest moments, everyone stayed positive. The family, the friends, doctors and nurses, all worked together, and the miracle child lived.
>
> This child touched all he met in a special way. People felt hope because of him. People learned to love, and value each moment. There were times as he grew when the parent felt a special presence surrounding him.
>
> As he began to speak, he often spoke to unseen friends he called the "soft people." Often, the "soft people" seemed to comfort him in the night or ease a scraped knee before the parents could get to him.

One night, he spoke to his mother of the "soft people." He described them as friends with shiny wings. One soft person is a little boy who plays with him and spends the night in his bed. Another is a little girl who tells stories and likes to play quietly when his heart is tired. There is an old grandmother who snuggles.

One of the secrets of this special small person that keeps him going and happy, when most would give up, is, as he says, he is surrounded by 'soft people' who are his special friends. His angels.

Carolyn and I find it impossible to imagine how anyone could read The Messengers and hear about the "soft people" from the mouth a three-year-old, and still doubt the existence of angels.

May God pour out his blessings upon you in this outer existence and those to come, for taking the risk to share your story with all of us.

Sincerely,
Mark L.

Nick read and reread the letter. The knowledge that the angels had helped this child, as they had helped Nick, verified what he had already known within himself: The Age of Wonders had begun. Throughout the ages, children have served as simple reminders to us how the Divine intervenes in our lives through these heavenly messengers. Had not Nick's memories of Jesus, as written in *The Messengers*, reminded him and the entire world that God dwells within each one of us?

Since the release of the book, mail from around the world had poured into his office. Many of those letters addressed personal issues, hopes, and aspirations. Many asked for help, others expressed the desire to volunteer help. All spoke of the inescapable feeling that hope once again was moving across the face of the Earth. However, it was one thing to speak of hope, and quite another to live it. Daniel was living evidence of that hope, living evidence of a new vision flowing forth, especially from the young, the future hope for our entire planet. Nick knew that the inevitable was now here: Humanity and the realm of angels once again would try to join the worlds of shepherds and kings to foster the emergence of everlasting peace.

Nick turned the letter over hoping there was more to read. Leaning back into his executive chair, he thought about what he was witnessing in his own little son, Nicholas. The tyke could mesmerize Daddy with unexpected moments of looking up from his toys, pointing his little hand to the ceiling and grinning with delight. "What do you see, Nicholas?" Nick would love to ask.

"Angels," would be his son's definitive response. His tiny hands would reach out as if invisible playmates were reaching for him. His boyish giggle left little doubt in Dad's mind that his child was being watched over. Yes, the children seem to know. Heaven and Earth are moving into Oneness.

Nick spoke little of what the angels had conveyed to him about what was to come to the people of the Earth. The bringing together of Heaven and Earth would not be like the mixing of eggs and flour for the baking of a cake. This was not going to be a merging of ingredients for the festivities of a birthday party. Far from it. No, Nick knew what he had been told would feed the soul, the heart, and the spiritual consciousness of all humanity. The angels had instructed him to be subtle about what he had heard from them. He was not to reveal the coming events, so people would not be tempted to focus on physical phenomena and be distracted from focusing on their own spiritual growth, their own capacity to love, their own journeys with self-truth.

Since the writing of *The Messengers*, Nick had started his journal of messages, which the angels were divulging to him on an ongoing basis. Significant events, stories, thoughts, and poems were added with these messages. Staring at the letter, he decided to photocopy it and add Daniel's story of the "soft people" to his journal. So much was happening around Nick. Letters such as this filled him with hope, inspiring him to continue his own remarkable journey.

After inserting Daniel's letter, his left hand rested on the journal. *It was all worth it*, he said to himself, his fingers rubbing the smooth cover as if reading angelic braille. His coming forward and revealing his personal story in *The Messengers* had prompted an outpouring of love, hope and inspiration found in the constant flow of mail into his offices. These thousands of letters from all over the world added further to the words, the dreams, the visions hidden in his journal. The angels were now saying that it was time to let people know what was coming, to tell the people of the Earth of the kind of world they were about to inherit. But when was the right time to speak of this? That was the question.

Almost unconsciously he opened the journal and began reading:

It is not the end of the world that is coming. It is the beginning of a new world. A world where people will recognize that happiness is not found in the accumulation of wealth and the wielding of power, or created through the motivations of greed and avarice. The world has created false expectations and false priorities that cannot be maintained. It is unfortunate, for the greatest reward one can have is that which comes from sharing love and compassion with others. If you give love and compassion to others, so shall you receive the same in return. If you plant an onion seed in your garden, you do not get a rose in return, but an onion. So it is with love.

The present offers little difference from the past. Throughout history, there has existed the need for people to have hope in their future and belief in their present. Your seniors, those who are your fathers and mothers, are living on fixed incomes. They have great fear in becoming a burden to their children and to society. Yet there is nothing they can do, for they have become spectators to a changing, confusing, consuming economy. What hope can they have in the tomorrow?

The young adults of today may not articulate the frustration of your present-day society, but their actions ring with greater clarity than any words. Many are choosing to live together in what would have been considered inappropriate in days past, rather than entering the convention of matrimony. They do not want to commit themselves to the standards that have gone before them. They are suspicious of the future, and many cast aside these old conventions. And you, who are among them, are not justified in finding fault with them, for they are in the beginning stages of their journeys. Can you not sense their frustration in your world?

You all are children of God, for the Lord is your Father and Mother. And what are the messages God wishes you to hear? Not

messages where love is turned to fear. Not messages of
compassion changed to messages of guilt. God wishes you to care
for one another as brothers and sisters.

People are searching for a true understanding of their
relationship to God, a relationship of mutual love and respect, not
one based on fear and punishment. Say to one another, 'Let us join
together as brothers and sisters in every state of our nation, in every
nation of the world, in a spirit of cooperation greater than ever
experienced in the history of humankind. Let us shout with joy our
heartfelt need to be at one with God. Let us help every child of God
in the world learn to enjoy the journey we travel together, in
becoming one with God.

"Nick, we have to make a decision about the print run." Gary
had quietly entered his office, interrupting his reading. Nick
looked up at his associate and friend, reflecting on how much the
two of them had gone through together in publishing *The
Messengers* in the Northwest. It had been a daunting task fraught
with unexpected obstacles, discouragement, and even frustration
at times. It was the price they had paid for bucking the system. But
it also proved to be rewarding beyond anyone's expectations —
except maybe Nick's.

"Gary, are you sure we need to decide now? We are starting to
get inquiries from some of the big publishing houses."

"If we don't decide within the week, we won't have enough
books for our national release in March."

Both men had taken different sides of the issue as to whether
they continue in their own efforts as a publisher, or whether they
take advantage of the rising interest being shown by the major
publishers. Gary would remind Nick of the timetable the angels had
presented, and Nick would remind Gary of the monumental tasks
before them, as well as the increasing workload that everyone in the
office was feeling.

"Let's not assume that a major house can't bring the book out
quickly," Nick offered. Gary's background in the publishing field
told him otherwise, but by this time in their weaving of efforts, Gary
had begun to respect Nick's uncanny instincts in the business world.

Gary had worked with Nick and Julia Ingram in writing the manuscript that would eventually become *The Messengers*. It had been a team effort all the way. The angels had given Nick a date when the book had to come before the public. And the only way to assure its exposure in a timely fashion was to self-publish — which meant that concentrated human resources and cash would be needed. It was an easy call for Nick at the time. Since it needed to be done, it *would* be done.

All of Nick's colleagues had supported him in his efforts of test marketing *The Messengers* in Seattle and Portland. If the angels said to publish in Seattle, then publish they would. There was a great sense of trust for what had been communicated from the angelic realm to those who surrounded Nick. The regional release of the book was a resounding success in spite of all the problems that had to be faced, in spite of all the obstacles inherent in a long-established book industry. An ingenious marketing campaign, meant to go around the book industry's lethargic system had worked. The book became the talk of the Pacific Northwest. News crews showed up to find out why a prominent, respected businessman was daring to tell people that angels had appeared to him — before witnesses — encouraging him to tell his story. Was he was the reincarnation of the spirit and soul of one of the most influential men in history: Paul the Apostle?

Sure, Nick heard derision and mumbling about having lost his mind. But he also heard heartfelt praise from people around the region who had heard his story, believed his sincerity, and trusted in the messages he had come to deliver — even messages that had been lost over the last 2,000 years. But what was equally captivating was the information the angels were conveying about the future, telling of a new kind of world enveloped in peace, compassion, and respect for all that is inherently good in humanity.

Nick's expected success of *The Messengers* had forced Gary to face the possibilities of Nick's vision for a greater world — what Nick liked to call "The Great Tomorrow." The time had arrived to move the book with its messages to a national, if not international level, and, as publisher, he was responsible for organizing an advertising campaign with Nick that would be ten times as complex as the Northwest endeavor. Then there were the matters of print runs, national distribution, publicity, and last but not least, the writing of the sequel. The angels had relayed that events would unfold around the turn of the millennium. Not only did *The Messengers* need to be made available to people but so did the accumulating information in Nick's journal. The two of them spoke often about the contents in this journal. Like the national campaign, both men had different ideas as to when and how this information should be brought forward.

One fact in particular Gary wanted kept secret. Sara, the angel seer, spoken of in *The Messengers*, had been the first to reveal the secret to Gary over the phone. It had shocked him at the time. Her telling Nick he had been Paul the Apostle wasn't such a big deal since Nick had been told several times already by others. But to compound that with news that Paul's "beloved" friend, Timothy, had incarnated at this time as well was just too much. Gary had been upset for days over this news. The implications disturbed his sense of responsibility as well as his obsession for the truth. How could this be true? Him? Saint Timothy? Sara had made a joke out of how Paul had a nickname for Timothy, "Timidus" — Timothy the Timid — and how that trait still held true in him. To make matters worse, Nick had entered Gary's office afterwards and had stated that Nick knew what was upsetting him. When Gary asked what, Nick stated, "I know you are the return of Timothy. I've known for quite a while."

One thing was obvious about a national campaign, both Nick and Gary needed help. Nick proposed hiring a man he greatly respected, Brian Hilliard. Gary had opposed bringing in Brian the first time Nick had suggested Gary share some of his workload. At the time, Gary felt too much was happening too fast to spend time training another person to finish what he had started. Nick had been patient. Though it was not his usual way, he had learned to let Gary make his own mistakes. Inevitably, he knew the two would speak with one voice, as before. Brian was brought on board with Gary handing over responsibilities to him the way a miser hands out his own gold, one coin at a time — and with reluctance.

Like little Daniel, Gary and Brian would come to know the "soft people" as Nick had. The angels were like ushers in the Theatre of

Life, helping key figures play their parts in creating a play of epic proportion. As Scripture so aptly puts it, "Who knows the mind of God?" Each of these men would participate in events that few humans are privileged to witness. Little did Brian and Gary know what was in store for them. Like other significant moments in his life, these two men would be added to Nick's angelic journal. And like an old story told millennia ago, they would help prepare the telling of another story that the Earth, herself, seemed anxious to hear.

As events would continue to unfold, it would be evident that no one, not modern-day prophets, not spiritual guides, not even the angels would know what was stirring within the cosmic soul of God. Nick's journal contained prophesies and stories, prayers and poems, thoughts and ideas. Anyone examining any single entry in Nick's journal would see nothing but a moment in time, a single frame in a mile of movie film. In Nick's journal, next to Daniel's story of the soft people, was scribbled a passage:

> There is a spiritual consciousness spreading throughout the world like never before in the history of mankind. Our minds are the gatekeepers of our hearts and souls, and a common voice is coming forth, threatening to break through those gates, shouting, "Let truth be heard." People from all walks of life are stepping out of the shadows and into the beauty of God's sunlight.

> We are the children of God, for the Lord is our Father and Mother. The Spirit of God that resides in each of us is beyond any person's greatest riches. No amount of money in the world, no amount of power or control of others can purchase that extraordinary gift, or take that gift from another. And with this understanding, as we enter the new millennium, we shall acknowledge all of God's children, all of our brothers and sisters. Not through greed, or envy, or jealousy, but with our hearts full of love and compassion.

> We live in a new Age of Wonders which will embrace spiritual leadership, and we shall learn to enjoy life every moment while letting others enjoy life through us.

As Nick continued to turn the pages of his "Angel Journal," he thought to himself, *Make no conclusions, forecast no future, and expect no predictable endings*, for, truly, who knows the mind of God? It will take the combined presence of the God-Within us all, the total consciousness of humankind, to reach a discernible conclusion as the last page of this angelic journal is turned. As these pages turn, so turn the stories of our own lives. What follows are stories which began as journal entries and evolved into a chorus of voices, a choir for the Age of Wonders. Neither Nick nor Gary would ever fully understand the unexpected paths their lives were about to take in finding these voices.

Listen, as your own soul is tempted to sing a new song with a million other souls because of what these pages hold. This chorus of souls is about to reveal what is to befall our world. Trust no single voice, but hear only the chorus of humanity singing in harmony with the chorus of angels — Peace on Earth, goodwill to all.

2

An Angel in New York

"Mad Dog!" Brian yelled across the suite offices. Nick had branded Gary with the nickname "Mad Dog" for reasons known only to Nick. It was tantamount to gracing Ghandi with the nickname of "Crusher." Without waiting for the normal "What's up?" Brian hurtled past Beth and Heather's offices into Gary's like a runner crossing a finish line. "You won't believe what just happened." Gary continued typing away on his laptop. The guy performed his office duties like a monk in prayer. Brian debated whether to throw a paper wad to get his attention. Just about the time Brian was cocking his arm to unleash his makeshift missile, Gary peered over his computer.

"How many guesses do I get?" Brian's eyes were as bright as searchlights. The shiny metal frames of his glasses only accented his excitement.

"Forget guesses." Brian would not be thwarted by his cohort's teasing delay tactics. The two were like confluent rivers, one forever rushing with rumbling rapids into the the stillness of the other. The course of their combined efforts could never be predicted. Every head in the office looked up, including Nick's. Whenever these two went at it, laughter was inevitable. "I just got off the phone with a New York publisher. They want our book, they want *The Messengers*, and they're ready to deal." Had not Sara, the "Angel Lady," told Nick that the angels predicted a major publisher would come forward to propel the story into the national limelight? Sara and Nick stayed in frequent contact. It had been through her that the original message had come forth about the angels announcing their presence with the number 444.

"So it's finally happened," Gary acknowledged, his mechanical pencil waving back and forth between two fingers. Brian grinned broadly, knowing the swaying pencil to be the height of emotional excitement from his colleague.

"They want us to come out there and meet with them. It's time to wheel and deal!" Gary sat quietly enthralled, studying Brian as he bubbled over like campfire coffee on hot coals. If his smile were any broader, they'd have to widen the door. But Gary remained uncertain now as he had when he and Nick had debated whether to finance their own national campaign or try to go with a major publishing house. It was time to check in with the angels.

That night Nick asked for confirmation from his angels as to whether their strategies were the best way to get the messages in the book before the world. Little Nicholas woke up fussing, in turn waking Dad via the intercom between the bedrooms. Nick tiptoed into his son's bedroom to make sure all was well. After tucking the infant in, he returned to bed snatching a look at the digital clock. It was 4:44 a.m. That was the sign he needed. Since the angels had first started communicating and appearing to Nick, they often used the number 444 to designate their presence, their love, their approval. Since the publishing of the book, hundreds of others from all parts of the country were likewise now seeing this angelic sign. Letters arrived daily telling funny, touching, and incredible stories, disclosing the ever-increasing presence of angelic forces upon the Earth. Grown-ups who weren't seeing the "soft people" were experiencing 444 encounters, realizing that their angels were indeed in their lives.

Having gotten the sign he had asked for that morning, Nick had Beth, his executive assistant (the real power behind the throne), arrange flight reservations to New York for the first week of March. Gary grumbled that he really wasn't needed in negotiations. Perhaps money should be saved by having him hold down the fort here at home.

"Mad Dog, you're going to New York with us," Nick insisted. "We need you to be the normal one, so we can wheel and deal. We'll wear our business suits while you wear a turtleneck. And you need a pipe. You should walk around with a pipe "

"No way," protested the blushing publisher. The truth of the matter was that Nick loved to see Gary blush. He went out of his way to see his friend radiate in crimson. All Nick's years of business deals had absolved him from the company of such near-innocence. Men in big business deals simply do not blush. Consequently, Nick would start chuckling the moment Gary's face reddened.

"Mad Dog," Brian teased, "We can't do this without you, big fella." It hadn't taken Brian long to appreciate the art of constant teasing that passed between the suite of offices. Even Beth was a pro. Poor Mad Dog never had a chance.

"Listen," Nick added, "I'll call the senior editor in New York and ask her if it's OK if you wear blue jeans and a sport coat with suede pads on the elbows." Before Gary's red could fade to pink, Nick's fingers had hit the quick-dial button and then the speaker phone button. Both Nick and Brian had wasted no time in operating on a first-name basis with the New York editor. Mad Dog's red was now heating up to vermilion. Even Brian had to turn away his grinned amazement at how close to purple Gary was flushing. There was only one ring on the other end.

"Hello, this is Lannie."

"Lannie, this is Nick Bunick."

"Well, hello, Nick. We were just talking about you and your marvelous book. You packed and ready to come to New York?

"Very much looking forward to it, Lannie. Very much. You remember Gary, our publisher and co-author? We're telling Gary that it's a must that he be at our New York meeting with you good folks. What do you think?"

"Absolutely," she crowed. She knew something was up for Nick to call her on such a mundane topic. She followed with the Jewish-mother side of her New York accent, "He's gotta be here."

"We think he should dress casually for the meetings, but he thinks otherwise." Brian silently shook, listening to Nick have his fun.

"Hey," Lannie echoed, now with an Italian accent, "he can wear a dress for all I care. This is New York!"

Both Nick and Brian were laughing openly. Beth leaned across her front desk to peer into Nick's office. What were "the boys" up to now? There was entirely too much fun going on. She knew Nick had to be up to his shenanigans. Gary's colorful face betrayed utter disbelief.

"A dress? Really?" Nick egged on. Brian's chair almost tipped over with exaggerated delight. Lannie could tell what was going on.

"You can't believe what we see here," Lannie continued. "We see all kinds of writers — men in dresses, women in see-through, long-haired male authors, baldheaded female authors ..." The bantering persisted. Even Brian joined in. Gary stared stoically.

The truth of the matter was that Nick had already grown to respect Lannie's people skills. She could carry on a conversation with seaweed. She was bright, loved to tell jokes, and better yet, she wanted the book. This kind of informal playfulness only endeared her more in his eyes. Gary, on the other hand, could not figure out how he could possibly show his face in New York.

"It's settled," Nick concluded as he hung up the phone. "We all go. Mad Dog, don't look so glum. We'll have a great time in New York."

Nick had come so far since first being told that his soul and spirit were, indeed, that of Paul the Apostle. Had not the angels urged him to let the world know? Like Paul on the road to Damascus, Nick's whole life had been changed by the angelic appearances and urgings. And now, he was no longer alone in what he saw. How soul-stirring that the little children also seemed to hold these divine beings as companions.

Looking forward, there seemed to be so much at stake. What could happen in New York might not only change Nick's life forever, it had implications for changing the lives of millions across the planet. It had been foretold this day was coming. And here it was at his doorstep. If he had only known how much detail the angels were eventually going to provide, he might never have made this trip. If he had only known how people, themselves, would change over the course of what was to come, he might have left the letter about the "soft people" filed away never to be seen again. And even if he had known of the upcoming changes, there would have been little he could have done to anticipate the power of human free will in altering the course of heavenly intent or human history. He should have been more attentive with the letter about little Daniel. For this lovely child was more than a warm story from proud parents; Daniel loomed as a prophetic metaphor of days to come.

Gary's hotel room resembled something out of a Carol Channing play: over-decorated, almost loud, but restful on the eyes in a forgotten way. In fact, the same could be said for much of New York. This was his first trip to the Big Apple, leaving him with a feeling that he had entered another era. To him, New York was simply an old and dirty city, but to Nick and Brian New York stood as the center of the business world, the Mecca of wheeling and dealing. Between the fortresses of commerce sparkled museums of some of the world's finest art, Broadway plays the rest of the country drooled over, and a fashion industry that instigated more chitchat than did Neanderthal football. Where else would the front page of the newspaper discuss the "taste" of the mayor dressed in drag for a benefit? Nick and Brian kept trying to enthuse Gary with walks down streets he had only seen in movies. Their efforts were wasted.

What impressed Gary the most was Nick's sauntering into St. Patrick's Cathedral at the noonday mass. In contrasting fashion, the dynamic duo of Brian and Nick respectfully tiptoed to one of the empty pews near the sanctuary while Gary stood silently in the vestibule absorbing the incredible beauty of the church architecture embracing human worship. Neither Nick nor Brian were Catholic, but it had now become part of their respect for all religions to visit a different church wherever they went. Even though Gary had studied for the priesthood at a Benedictine monastery, he viewed everything before him with arms folded and lips pursed. His were not fond memories.

Afterwards, the three stood on the cathedral steps staring at the towering spires. "Mad Dog, have you ever been to a real Jewish deli?" Nick asked, as Brian grinned widely at the hint of another adventure.

"I've been to a deli, and even a kosher deli, but I'm not sure whether I could actually say I'd been to a Jewish deli."

"Follow me. You're going to have a new experience." It seemed as if Nick had to cram as much excitement into the day as was humanly possible. All three men were slated to have their first meeting with the publishing house the next morning. The other interested publishers would be visited the following two days. Why Nick even tolerated Gary's reclusive tendencies was beyond reason, at least to Gary. If they had left him sitting in the hotel room with nothing more than a paperback novel and a TV remote, he would have been satisfied. To him, Brian and Nick were like whirlwinds kicking up dust in a faded city. But neither was to be denied. *If they show this much energy in the negotiations tomorrow morning*, Gary thought, *then pity poor Lannie.*

The Jewish deli was a sitcom. The men behind the counter were yelling instructions like quarterbacks barking out signals — all quarterbacks, no linemen. And Nick joined right in, throwing menu questions into the huddle of food handlers. What puzzled Gary was that all the men behind the counter were Latino, probably Puerto Rican. At least that's what it looked like to him. He had somehow pictured men in yarmulkes and prayer shawls. Brian's eyes widened brightly with amusement as he tried to toss in an order. In the end, Gary had to admit that his reuben sandwich was the best he had ever tasted. If this was typical New York, then he was beginning to like it.

That evening the three men had scheduled a meeting with a potential freelance publicist in the hotel cocktail lounge. They wanted someone who knew the New York crowd, someone who knew the ins and outs of the local book industry. After Gary made his pitch as publisher, he sat back and listened to Nick ask strategy questions.

Stefanos delivered his three newfound friends in the middle of the giant skyscrapers guarding America's publishing empire.

Security guards phoned Lannie. Gary made a silent bet with himself how long it would take the elevators to deliver the senior editor from forty floors up. "Nick?" she asked as she walked out of the elevator. *He is even more dynamic in person,* she thought to herself.

"Lannie!" Nick returned, as if he had found a long-lost friend. She almost disappeared in the crush of his hug. Gary hung in the background as the two suits began what would be an unforgettable day.

"Gary?" Lannie chimed as she spotted the blue jeans. Her smile was genuine and her handshake warm. On the phone, she had seemed so stalwart, large in spirit, a woman of powerful persuasion. But here, she looked more like a petite nun in designer garb, dressed impeccably. If the truth be known, Lannie loved shopping for clothes almost as much as she loved books.

"It's a pleasure to meet you," Gary managed, without even blushing. *Marian the Librarian meets John Boy Walton in jeans,* he couldn't help thinking.

Lannie herded the gaggle of men into a waiting elevator, whisking them away to the highest floors of authority. The first pleasantries were exchanged with executives. Different levels of editors huddled chairs together as verbal posturing began in the most sophisticated of ways. What a contrast to the streets below, where waving arms of doormen played chicken with brigades of yellow cabs. Up here, on the 40th-something floor, the greatest weapon was the tongue. And Gary knew enough to leave the talking to Nick. Absolving himself of responsibility, Gary's eyes wandered to the rooftops across the way. From up here, New York looked even older and dirtier. Yet, inside the office buildings, the creative forces of the known world were fostering new revelations of knowledge. For centuries, the common book awakened humans to new possibilities, new lives, new loves, and new worlds. Despite all the wonders that centers of technology displayed in other cities, shiny and clean with their glassy exteriors, it was here among the dusty buildings of New York, like so many dusty bookshelves, that real power reigned — the power of the human mind.

The next round of discussions moved to the conference room. The three men sat together on one side of an immense table while all the top managers and executives surrounded them. Brian's eyes were beginning to dance. These were all women. All seven of them. No men, except the three guys. What a statement. There was obviously no glass ceiling here. Brian wondered if Nick would be able to handle this kind of feminine power. After all, Nick was used to the corporate muscling that typically occurred in most male-dominated industries. For that matter, what about himself? Should he handle his own presentation any differently? It was his turn to give the marketing picture. He decided it should be given no differently.

As negotiating wound down, the executives finally said what Nick wanted to hear. "OK, what would it take to get you to cancel your other publisher appointments? We want this book."

Up to this point, Gary had been counting coffee mugs and noting the different sayings on them. These women were not only funny, their coffee mugs even betrayed a bawdy side. *This must be a fun place to work*, Gary thought as he half-heard Nick's response. Up to this point, Mad Dog had been window dressing in a showcase display.

"Gary. What do you think?" Nick posited, as he leaned over on the hardwood table staring down at his publisher. "What would it take for you to give these wonderful people our book?"

All eyes turned to Gary with one singular motion. What did Nick think he was doing? Had he not told Gary to let him do all the talking? Brian mentally took note that this was the first time he saw Gary go white instead of red. Stalling for a little time, he swallowed the remainder of water in his glass, hoping not to choke. "Well, I like everything I've heard here," he confessed softly. "I can't think of better people to go with than the people I've seen here." His eyes rested on Lannie. She smiled back. What he was hoping for was some kind of hint from Nick or Brian. However, he was on his own. "We need to have this book out fast because of the importance of the messages within. The only way this industry will take this book seriously is if we strike a deal for seven figures."

Nick's eyes turned to the person who had the power to say yes or no. His business mind delighted how Gary had said just the right thing. Nick loved to trust his instincts.

"I don't know if we can do that," replied one of the executives. Counteroffers were made, but Nick knew he had the upper hand, and knew how to use it.

After a span of silence one of the executives turned to the senior editor, "Lannie, why don't you take these gentlemen to lunch." Then turning to the publishing house president she finished, "while I see if I can get an answer before they leave today."

Everyone stood up, exchanged compliments, and emptied the room. Lannie hustled the guys into her office, searching for enough chairs to fit into her nun's cell. The only thing missing was a flat cot and a crucifix hanging on the wall. It was almost austere. As Lannie made arrangements on the phone, chatting in between holds, Gary began to notice a figure appearing behind the editor. A chill of goose bumps swept him as he began to see what was unmistakably an angel. This was not the first time one of these beings had appeared before him. And like before, he froze in place, mesmerized by the silent figure. This angel even had wings. When this had happened before, he had seen a robe of light and a featureless countenance. As Nick and Lannie were going over contractual concerns, Nick noticed the strange look on his friend's face.

"Mad Dog? You OK?"

Gary could not take his eyes off the vision. What was this angelic figure doing here? What did it mean?

"Mad Dog? Are you comfortable with our decision here?" Gary had not even heard what the decision was. He knew well enough to let Nick handle contractual discussions.

"Uhh, yes, I'm fine with it. Fine." The angel did nothing nor said nothing. It just stood behind Lannie with a peaceful look on its face. Its shape was not distinctive, almost like looking at a reflection in a department store window. *One of the soft people,* Gary said to himself. His mind fought with what to do, what to say. There was nothing that could be done or said. Lannie would surely think him fanciful, or perhaps think him unstable. However, this appearance had to be a good sign. It had to mean they were negotiating with the right publisher, and Lannie the right editor for this book. But nothing was hinted at by the ghostlike figure. Only silence.

What a contrast this was to the children who openly acknowledged these "soft people." Grown-ups too afraid to admit the divine, were here to prepare a world for children who talked with these beings, reached out to them, accepted them without reserve. What is it about being "grown up" that denies us our own deep truths? What kind of message do we send, what kind of world do we foster if we espouse the wonders of heaven yet say nothing when it makes its presence known? This kind of silence is not "golden," it is made of lead, and it weighs us down as we continue to deny the marvels of an emerging world, a world made finer by human acknowledgment of the divine. Gary would realize later what this angelic presence meant, and only then would he confess to what he had witnessed this day.

While Lannie hustled the crew down the elevator for a springtime walk to one of New York's finer establishments, she and Nick bantered back and forth about the meeting. "Does anyone else smoke?" she asked politely as they cruised through the islands of bodies along the sidewalk.

"No, but go ahead, Lannie. We're outside in the fresh air," Nick volunteered.

She wrinkled her nose, "Oh, no, I don't want be bothering anyone else."

"I can walk in front of you, and listen at the same time," Gary added. Brian walked beside him whispering how well he thought the meeting went. Gary was only half-listening, for he could still see the angelic figure behind Lannie. He leaned over into Brian's ear. "We have company," he whispered above the crowd noise.

Brian looked around as if expecting a Mafia figure to appear. "What do you mean?" he whispered back.

"You know ..." Gary decided this was not a good idea. Brian wondered what was going on. There had been several dropped hints on the part of Nick and Gary over the past several weeks that prompted Brian to wonder if the two men had some private secret, or private joke that only the two of them enjoyed.

Brian stared over at Nick who, at this point, was joining Lannie in smoking a cigarette. Nick wasn't a smoker. *What is he doing?* Brian wondered. A chuckle gurgled up from inside as he remembered the episode in the cab earlier that morning. Had Nick not insisted that Stefanos, the cab driver, throw out his cigarette because the foul air was bothering Gary. He decided to nudge Gary while nodding his head to the right in the direction of Nick. His companion craned his neck to see Nick barely puffing away, obviously making Lannie feel comfortable.

"That Nick," Gary smiled. "He really is just like Paul."

"What do you mean?" Brian asked.

" 'I am all things to all men,' " Gary quoted from Paul's first letter to the Corinthians.

Brian's eyes jumped back and forth between Nick and Gary as if he were watching a tennis match. Not knowing what else to say, he smilingly questioned, "You OK, Mad Dog?"

"I'm OK, Bri." Gary was beginning to develop a fondness for this new guy. He had an ease about him that transcended business as well as the personal. "I'm OK." Gary knew the angel had to be a favorable sign. Certainly all was well. Or so he thought. Later that day, contracts were signed and deals made, but some matters cannot be written into seven-figure contracts — like certain secrets of the heart.

"Nicky, I have a personal favor to ask you," Lannie's voice entreated tenderly. Thousands of miles of phone line could not hide her effort to disguise her feelings. However, Nick could read people the way Lannie speed-read books. His eyes looked far away beyond his office window as if bird-dogging the phone lines back to the source of this gentle voice. The contracts had been signed in New York, and the month that followed had brought him and Lannie closer as business contacts as well as friends.

"Lannie, you OK?" was his patented response. He was buying time. These were no longer business associates talking. Lannie was far more than an editor, and she no longer thought of Brian, Gary, and Nick as clients. All had become unexpected friends. Whenever Nick or Lannie wanted to make a point that transcended business or get to the heart of an issue, they would abandon any formalities and speak to each other in the familiar. When matters got tense, for whatever reason, it was not "Ms. Editor" nor "Mr. Bunick" that was resorted to. Quite the opposite. They became "Nicky" and "Lannie." No matter how far apart they were on any contract or business issue, "Nicky" and "Lannie" would inevitably end up laughing. Sometimes there might be a few tears before the laugh line, but they would end up laughing, nonetheless. There was no business matter that could not be resolved; there was no personal issue that could not be shared.

The hanging silence finally surrendered, "I'm OK, Nicky. I'm OK. But my best friend, Suzette, isn't. She's been diagnosed with terminal cancer. She has cancer, and doesn't have long to live." She could barely finish the sentence before tears tried to ease her choking words. Her heart was breaking. Lannie loved people. There was no other word for it. She simply loved people, from closest friends to the homeless woman whom she called her "street angel." Sometimes, while Lannie waited for her bus, this crumpled old woman would sidle up alongside and begin a conversation. The disheveled old lady might talk about the smells of the street or the weather. But she would more often than not talk about something that seemed to make no sense at the time, only to make perfect sense later. Angels, she would point out, it was angels who were following Lannie. If Gary had only known. But at this moment Lannie could not feel blessed by the presence of an angel.

"Has she gotten a second opinion?" Nick asked, still buying time. He was sniffing the air for what really was agonizing the tenderhearted Lannie.

"No, but she is going to. I can't believe this has happened. She is such an alive and good person." Nick began to realize what Lannie was trying to do.

"You said you had a favor to ask?" He gave her an opening.

"Nick, I know you get all kinds of requests from people who want you to help them. And I don't want to burden you with this. But I have to ask you this. Suzette is so dear to me. Could you pray to your angels to heal her of the cancer?"

Nick leaned back in his executive chair, his hand resting against his cheek. This was a sensitive topic. He knew that his purpose for being on earth this time around was different than the purpose of Paul of Tarsus 2,000 years ago. Though healing had been a large factor in bringing people closer to the truth of God in those days, it was not the focus of his life now. For one thing, it would be too easy for healing to become a media phenomenon. And that could easily get in the way of why he was here now. It would be too easy for it to become a distraction to the real truth: We are our own best healers. It was paramount that people realize that God is within each one of us. That was the message two millennia ago, but did people remember it?

"Lannie, here's what I will do. I will ask the angels to intervene. But I want you to do the same. Do you understand?"

"Of course," came the hopeful reply.

"We cannot interfere in people's lives. We must respect their own journey. It simply may be Suzette's time to move on into spirit. She may have accomplished what she came here to do. And we have to accept that, if it is so."

"I know, Nick. But I can't believe her time is over. She has so much to give people."

"All right. I want you to tell your friend we both will talk to our angels. But I want you to tell her to constantly remind herself that God is within her. Have her spend time forgiving herself for any wrongs she feels she may have committed. Have her open herself to God's love. OK?

"I'll call her right away."

That night the two friends opened their hearts in prayer to God and to the angels. This was not a matter of begging for a miracle. It was an act of trust that the love flowing between these people would benefit another, no matter what the outcome. These were not prayers of supplication, these were prayers of acknowledgment, of oneness between humanity and angels. This was not an effort to cheat death, it was a common recognition that we are all fully to embrace life. And if that means that life is to pass from the body and follow spirit, then so be it. There was nothing more to do than wait. Pray and wait.

Brian and Gary were having one of their typical afternoon strategy sessions in Brian's office, covering the white-board in red lines, blue words, and green graphics. Everyone was now working together to come up with the best way to take *The Messengers* before the general public. A beep hiccuped on the office phone.

"Brian, it's New York," announced Heather, who used the intercom only to interrupt, then would yell across the office suites like everyone else. "I think it's Lannie." Gary took a seat next to Brian's credenza so both men could hear over the speakerphone. Brian hit the button in comic fashion. She was probably going to give him grief over one of his marketing ideas.

"Lannie!" Brian cheered, to start the conversation. Only a sniffle could be heard on the speaker.

"Lannie, you OK?" Gary kidded, using Nick's patented joke. Again there was no response. Brian leaned toward the phone, his eyes asking Gary what could be wrong.

"Lannie, this is Brian. Is everything OK?"

"No ... yes," a choked voice returned. "Nick is busy on the phone, talking to London. I had to talk to somebody."

Again Brian's eyes flashed a what-am-I-going-to-do look at Gary. "Is there something I can do? Just say the word. I'm here for you." It was classic Brian. He would give the shirt off his back to a stranger. In fact, he'd give the shirt off his back to anyone who needed it. No accident that he was one of the forces behind the creation of Night Watch, a support organization for street people in the Portland area, established to help the homeless.

"You guys, I'm not sure what to say. You know my friend, Suzette, I told you about? The one diagnosed with cancer?"

Both men chimed, "Yes."

"Well, I had asked Nick if he would ask his angels to help heal her. He asked me to do the same. Well, Suzette went to go for tests today, for a second opinion. They sent her home. They couldn't find any cancer." The word "cancer" was almost inaudible as Lannie sobbed uncontrollably. Gary knew she had been heartsick at the thought of losing her best friend.

"What happened in the doctor's office?" Gary wanted to know.

Still choking back her words, Lannie continued, "The physician said she had been misdiagnosed. He said the only thing he could see was small fractures in her bones. He didn't see her like I did for the last two months. This wasn't a misdiagnosis. She could hardly move, there was no life in her, she was dying, for God's sake." Again the sobs poured over the phone line. Brian stared out the window with a gaze that made you wonder if he was watching God. Gary simply covered his face. His own emotions were being tested these last couple of days.

"So, she's OK now?" Gary asked, feeling just a little stupid asking.

"She's doing great. She's laughing, she's walking around. The color has returned to her face. I can't believe it. Last week she looked gray, could barely get out of bed. She was dying. I don't care what anyone says, I know Nick is responsible for this happening."

Gary knew that Nick would be the first to correct Lannie, even in her tears of joy. So he decided to speak for his friend. "Now Lannie, Nick would quickly remind you that it was the angels who were asked to help in the healing."

"He's the one who prayed to his angels," she countered.

"If memory serves me correctly, you also prayed to your angels. No?"

"Well, yes."

"Then don't discount your own role in this. Healing comes from within. And you probably played a stronger role than anyone in helping Suzette open to her own healing."

Nick was quite willing to take people through what he called "healing of the spirit." But he wanted everyone to understand that such an exercise addressed the spirit, firstly and foremost. He wanted people to understand the strong connection between our spiritual state and our physical state. In no way, shape, or form, did he want people to see him as the healer Jeshua was. And even Jeshua constantly told people that they were the healers, not he. At this time in history, Nick's role was to get people to remember. Remember the original messages of Jeshua. Remember that God is within us all. Remember that we are called to live a life of universal love, compassion, and to live in truth.

"Yes, I know you are right," Lannie returned. "But I am still holding Nick responsible." A small laugh tripped across the speakerphone. Brian continued to stare out the window. No one wanted to hang up. The electric feeling of wonder filled the space between New York and Portland. *Wow*! they all wanted to say. But no one could speak. *We have entered the Age of Wonders*, they wanted to say. But no one said anything. The truth of the matter was that Gary couldn't speak anyway. He sat there so choked up he had to just get up from his chair and leave Brian's office. With head hung, as if searching for invisibility, he grabbed his laptop from his office and left the building. It was too much. This was all getting to be too much. Was this really happening? Were we, as a people, truly coming out of our woundedness? For the first time in his life, Gary wanted to find a quiet, secret place, just to see if he could talk to his angels. He wanted to thank them for this life surrounding him. *This must have been what it was like 2,000 years ago, only better*, he thought. *For this time, our race, our civilization just might get it right. This time, we just might remember Jeshua's key message: God is within each one of us.* Gary drove away carrying his silence and his recognition of God within him. There was simply nothing to be said.

3

OUT OF WOUNDEDNESS

We can be such a foolish people; we can be such a glorious people. The glory of what we can create is rivaled only by our power to destroy. How often has the world witnessed miracles, only later to destroy the miracle workers? What is in us that is so reluctant to embrace our own wonder? As with any age, the telling visions of our children can be obliterated by the denial within ourselves. It was as if heaven knew ahead of time that some phenomenon would have to be in place to counter our tendency as a people to deny the simple, honest truth that stands in front of us. And Nick Bunick was no exception to this tendency. His own denial, his own concerns over ridicule and family safety nearly thwarted his very purpose for being here. Had it not been for the presence of angels in his own life, we might never have been allowed the awareness of coming events that will rival history.

More and more requests for appearances arrived at Nick's offices. He tried to answer each letter personally but the volume was rapidly getting beyond his capability to do so. Hundreds of letters a week now made it impossible for even Nick's staff to help in this effort. However, one letter stood out among the rest. The letter was from a Reverend Georgie Richardson, pastor of a vibrant church, where people teach one another to expect miracles. Would Nick be willing to come down to Salem, Oregon, and speak before her congregation? *The Messengers* was already causing a bit of a stir among her congregation. And to further her enthusiasm, Reverend Richardson revealed that 444 events were unfolding in her own life. Nick discussed the idea with Gary, and the two of them decided to make a pilgrimage down to Georgie's church. Gary wanted to see how Nick would do in front of people who might have questions, who might press him for information that might push against their own religious convictions.

As Gary steered Nick's Jaguar onto the church grounds, both men grinned at seeing a welcome sign reserving a parking place for the two of them. And a good thing, too. The parking area was jammed. Gary barely missed one of the other cars as he tried to squeeze the unfamiliar Jag into the tight reserved spot. Nick teased, "Mad Dog, you OK?" He had Mad Dog drive the entire trip so that he would be rested and focused for what was about to unfold. This day was important to Nick, for it would be the beginning of what would be a new life for this former businessman and venture capitalist.

"Welcome," came the cheery voice, catching Gary by surprise. In his effort to slide the window down, he inadvertently turned on the windshield wipers. Finally conquering the cockpit technology of the Jaguar, Gary pressed the switch descending the window with a whine.

"Thank you," came his his belated reply.

"You must be Nick," she added, bending down to see the gentleman on the passenger's side.

"Yes, we're pleased to be here. And this is Gary, co-author of *The Messengers.*" Nick gestured with confidence.

"Hi," was all Gary could usher. He was blushing bright red again, wondering what this distinguished lady must be thinking of his klutzy battle with the car switches.

"I'm Georgie," she smiled while offering a hand.

I'm going to like this place, thought Gary. *Not Reverend Richardson, not even Reverend Georgie. Just Georgie.* Anxiously, Gary leaned halfway out the window to shake hands. Of course, his leaning inadvertently set off the window switch sending the blade of window up in reverse guillotine fashion. A Three Stooges move just managed to stop his being beheaded. Nick decided to exit before Mad Dog accidentally killed himself, grinning at the thought of an imaginary headline: "Local Author Strangled by Jaguar."

"Georgie, it was so good of you to invite us," Nick offered. Her knee-length dress fluttered bright flowerlike colors as she walked over to shake hands. Gary escaped from the menacing Jaguar unnoticed by anyone, saved from further threat. Taking a deep breath, he stared out at the waves of green meadow surrounding the church.

Reverend Richardson gathered her flock, for it was time to begin services. Nick would be the featured speaker during the liturgy, plus he would speak after lunch before a crowd wanting to hear his story and perhaps hear about the new world promised by the angels. Many wanted to know what the angels had said to him, what was coming that would change the planet forever. It was one thing to hope for an era of peace across the globe, and quite another to find out what it was going to take to get there.

Standing in front of the packed building, Georgie's eyes beamed with pleasure at the attendance. Her own elegance commanded respect as the gathering quieted to hear her blessing. All heads bowed.

"Thank you, God, for the wonder of your grace in my life," she said. "Can you imagine playing a game that you could not possibly lose, or take a test you could never fail? Because of the grace of God that has been given to us, we are assured that we can never fail — even if we feel we have. Each experience, whether completely successful or not, is a chance to learn and grow. So let's be joyous recipients of God's grace and accept the pure, the unconditional love that we have been so freely given. Through this love, we are nurtured and blessed. As we rise higher and higher in spiritual understanding, we joyfully embrace the many-faceted splendor of God's grace in action around us. With peace in our hearts we gratefully say, 'Thank you, God, for the wonder of your grace in our lives.' And from John 11:40: 'Did I not tell you that, if you believe, you would see the glory of God?' "

Georgie had captured the spirit of the gathering from the get-go. All eyes were focused on Nick as she related her own 444 experiences, how she had written the letter that had touched his heart, how blessed she felt for herself and her people that they were among the first witnesses to see the return of such a commanding spiritual figure as this man who was the soul and spirit of Paul the Apostle. Her directness, her lack of apology for daring to accept such a notion filled the air with a kind of magic. Indeed, the air vibrated with electricity as the gathering heard their pastor announce the beginning of a new Age of Wonders, what *The Messengers* had called "The Return of the Age of Miracles." Had they not already witnessed miraculous beginnings in their own lives? Her thanks to God had been genuine, unquestionably devout and direct.

Georgie next introduced a younger woman, named Mary Ann, a pianist/vocalist, who had composed a special song for the gathering, about Nick's journey. Mary Ann edged nervously on her piano bench as she introduced her creation. "I call this song *Nick's Song*, but it's everybody's song. It's about all our journeys, as we open to guidance, in the many forms it comes to us." Her hands hung suspended on the keys as if waiting for the song to sing itself.

With eyes shut, the first chord announced the beginning of Nick's journey, a journey that would eventually span the globe. As her words grew in feeling and intensity along with the music, Nick's eyes began to redden. Gary did a double-take. His friend and cohort, affected by a song? *It must be the power of the moment*, he mused. This entire community of well-wishers had pulled out the stops to welcome the both of them. Gary was struck by the irony of how removed he felt from the affection and the anticipation of the congregation, while Nick sat silently rapt in its sincerity and tenderness. As the song ended, Nick wiped the tears from his eyes. *I should get a picture of this*, Gary joked to himself. It was as if Nick knew that this was the beginning of living out the very reason he had been born. These people reflected a beauty that would ultimately capture the world. And he felt it, knew it.

As sniffles around the room quietly responded to soft tissues, Georgie stood before her people once again. She reflected on how she had come to write the letter that had brought Nick to their house of worship. In a voice that might remind one of a Mother Teresa, Georgie looked toward Gary and Nick, and claimed before her congregation, "And so we have Gary and Nick with us here today.

Like many, when I read *The Messengers*, I became very excited. Nick is a prominent Northwest businessman, and he's known since 1977 that he embodies the soul and the spirit of the Apostle Paul. Nine different spiritually-gifted people, at different times, have told him about that. And what a struggle it was for him to make this public, to go before people with this information. But then the angels got involved and started pushing on him, and he did take that next step. And we are so grateful, because there are many of you that have come up to me and have said, 'Georgie, this book has changed my life.' So it's such a pleasure to have him here today."

Both Nick and Gary were surprised by the eruption of applause. Neither had heard such a large sound in a place of worship. Nick entered the sanctuary, and stood nearly transfixed before the heralding, visibly moved. Yes, it had begun. And there was no turning back. Gary reached down to retrieve his notebook. He knew this was a moment that needed remembering.

With a confidence that seemed ancient, Nick enthralled his listeners with his spellbinding story, balancing the wonders of today against the truths of two millennia. Gary tried to sneak peeks at those around him, but felt too obvious in his efforts, for every eye was frozen on his friend. Never did he imagine that Nick would be this effective, or the people so welcoming. This moment was meant to be. Nick nourished the assembly with incident after incident of how the angels had convinced him that all of us are reentering the Age of Wonders.

"There are many other stories that I can tell," he summarized, "but I wanted to share with you these particular stories so that you might remember that the angels *are* the messengers of God, and are in every one our lives. Every one of us. They intervened in my life for a specific purpose because they wanted me to act. However, I am now aware that they have been inspiring me throughout my life, helping me at times when I needed help, giving me courage at times when I needed courage, giving me love at times when I didn't know how to find love on my own effort. And they're in all of your lives, also.

"Think of my story as your story — a key that will open for you a treasure chest everyone has inside of them. All you have to do is turn the key and open that treasure chest, taking that gift from God, knowing that you will have access to a wealth of riches never before realized. And those riches will be your ability to have direct communications with your angels. Even though it took me a while to realize this, it doesn't need to take you so long. I can tell you are much more open than I was."

With a humbleness and sincerity that surrendered to a charisma of love, Nick blessed the people with a benediction, encouraging them to follow the path that is theirs. Gary wanted to write notes about what he was witnessing, but the truth of the matter was that he couldn't take his eyes off the scene before him. Something had happened in Nick, something big. A chill went up Gary's spine as his companion returned to his seat, giving Gary's left hand a squeeze. *Nick isn't a hand-squeezer,* he thought. *Maybe the angels have snatched his real body,* he grinned at the thought. No, this was not the time to whisper in his ear, "Nick, you OK?" This was a moment to cherish. No matter how uncomfortable it made Gary, he knew that Nick had found his chosen path, his true calling.

Reverend Georgie closed the services with a meditation and a song. Afterwards, no one left the building. All were a hive of bees buzzing with excitement. Nick would speak again after lunch. Were seats still available? How was the afternoon seminar going to be different than the homily during the service? Their questions and comments filled the air with a hum of exhilaration.

While Nick was swarmed with well-wishers, Gary, as he was prone to do, tried to hide in his chair, arms folded and head bowed. His efforts to remain invisible proved futile as one of the members of the church, a Dr. Bonnie Young sat next to him and introduced herself. A middle-aged woman with a handsome face and nicely done hair, she spoke with pride about her community — how it had grown over the last three years, how the walls had to be broken down to make more room, how the offices had to be moved out into the trailer in the parking lot to accommodate even more growth. *Yes,* Gary thought, *this was a place where walls are broken down. Even mine.*

As the squeeze of people eased, Reverend Richardson rescued her guests for a relaxing lunch in her office. As she spread a feast before them, Nick took the occasion to question the make-up of Georgie's community. He did not want to offend anyone, especially his gracious host. In particular, Nick wanted to address Georgie's congregation, discussing the role of fear in the world, and more specifically the entire notion of hell and Satan. Georgie assured Nick that her people were quite open-minded to many concepts from many religions. Her house of God was a house that allowed all to enter. It was not uncommon for them to study from the *Koran*, the *Bible*, the *Book of Mormon*, or the *Bhagavad Ghita*. In her church, the only requirement was openness and tolerance for all who searched for God. She was not surprised to hear that Nick did not believe there was a hell, nor that there was a devil named Satan.

Georgie reassured Nick *The Messengers* had already made it apparent that Jeshua did not teach of hell as a place, nor Satan as a devil. She understood that Nick believed these to be inventions of a medieval church that chose to rule its people by fear rather than love. He asked Georgie if she was aware of the word "Gehenna," the premise for the notion of hell. Had she heard that it was, in reality, a garbage dump outside the city of Jerusalem. Indeed, she had heard such a notion while at seminary.

Gary sat back in his chair as he began to recall one of the recorded hypnotic-regression sessions that Nick and Julia had taped after the writing of *The Messengers*. Once again, Julia had taken Nick back 2,000 years to his life as Paul the Apostle. Gary remembered how Nick had played the tape back for him, how amused he became at hearing how "Gehenna" was a joke among the people of that day:

Julia (J):   I have a question about the city of Jerusalem itself.

Paul (P):   Yes.

J: Did Jeshua talk about a place called "Gehenna"? Do you have any information as to what that was?

P: I don't know if Jeshua talked about it, but there was such a place. Gehenna was outside Jerusalem below the road, as if you were going to Joppa, going towards the sea. It was below the road and was in the Hinnom Valley. ["Gehenna" comes from the original Hebrew "ge hinnom," which meant "valley of Hinnom." Nick, personally, had no knowledge of this fact.]

J: Go ahead.

P: Well, it was a place where people would take their things they no longer had use for [a dump]. There were people employed there by the officials who would keep it burning. It was a place they took things they no longer wanted and they burnt them there. And it was sloped in such a manner that it was in this valley. It was high on one side, the side towards Jerusalem, and lower on the side away from Jerusalem, so the smoke would not go back towards the city. That was the way the valley was shaped. It was a place where a lot of cistern canals led [carrying away sewage] because of the slope of the ground. And the people who were responsible for collecting refuse in the city would take the refuse by horse and cart and leave it there to be burnt. Gehenna.

J: So did it have a kind of an odor to it?

P: Oh yes [a smile comes across Nick's face]. It was a bad odor. People would insult each other when they would get angry, or when mothers got angry at the children, and the children misbehaved they would say "I'm going to send you to Gehenna if you do not behave." So it became almost like a joking curse.

It was a joke that history distorted over time. However, children were no longer the butt of this joke. "The fires of Gehenna" eventually became the premise for the concept of hell as we know it today. Nick wanted to make sure that Jeshua's message was no longer distorted. There was no hell, nor was there a devil, except the ones we choose to create for ourselves. Over millennia, people had been made to fear God because of such a notion. It angered Nick that anyone should be made to fear a God of love. It was not Jeshua's way to create fear in anyone. Quite the opposite. The way out of woundedness, all woundedness, was through love, compassion, and forgiveness.

Gary enjoyed the smoked salmon as well as the conversation between Nick and Georgie. There was a mutual respect that warmed the air. To make sure there would be no misunderstandings or religious differences Nick previewed some of what he wanted to address on the topic of Satan.

"If you go back and look at the Old Testament, there are references where we have the Israelite armies referring to their opponents as 'satans' — meaning evil people, monsters. As we might refer to the Nazis during World War II as devils, they would refer to the enemy as 'satans' in their behavior. They were evil people. What happened over the years is that this concept of satan was changed. Instead of conveying a sense of evilness, it began to take on the embodiment of evil, as if an entity. Unfortunately, it began to be used in the gospels through various stages of translation. Jeshua did not cast out demons, as entities. He cast out attitudes or states of being within a person. Back in the time of Pythagoras and Plato, hundreds of years before Jeshua was born, they referred to people who had attributes in their personalities that were bad — such as jealousy, envy, anger, hostility, greed — as 'daemons.' Meaning they have these unpleasant parts in their personalities. When Jeshua drove daemons out of people's hearts and souls, he was taking away from them this maliciousness they might have toward their fellow man or even toward themselves. But what happened over a period of time, was that the concept of daemon was changed to the word "demon." And with the change in word came a change in concept. This was *not* the concept of Jeshua and Paul," Nick insisted.

The primary reason for Nick's review of these ideas was to show people in the afternoon session how to find a place of healing for themselves. And that place of healing had to rest upon the notion of self-forgiveness and letting go of fear. Scripture was adamant in stating "Where there is fear there is not love." And Nick wanted the world to be reminded of Jeshua's desire for all people to understand that they walked with love, for God is within. And God is love.

Georgie's comments were as dynamic as Nick's. Gary listened to the two, reminded of scholars from ancient times discussing moral issues in Solomon's Temple. Were not good works as important as good words? Georgie offered. Were not Jeshua's messages hung on the branch of action as well as the branch of moral thought? Did they not come from the same tree? Georgie's had steeped her life in good works. She practiced what she preached. Gary made a point to interrupt his silence to accent what Georgie was bringing to the discussion, for was not Nick's concept of a greater tomorrow to be based on that very point that Georgie stood for? Besides, it would give Nick a chance to talk about his vision of the Great Tomorrow.

After making his point, Gary moved from the smoked salmon to the plate of assorted cookies as Nick and Georgie continued their lively discussion. Life was to be enjoyed to the full, and he was enjoying himself in the company of these two marvelous souls. Besides, he never met a chocolate chip cookie he didn't like. Georgie's nurturing eyes spied the empty cookie plate as her guest munched the last of the homemade cookies. While listening attentively to Nick, she quietly reached behind her for the container holding more of the booty, filled the empty plate, and gestured politely for Gary to help himself to more, never missing a word. Gary felt as if he were at home instead of a church complex.

"I was at a talk show recently, in Seattle," Nick said, "where a person called in to challenge me. His name was John, and John protested, 'How can you say what you're saying and claiming to be who you are, while at the same time not taking the Scriptures literally?' He said, 'You're wrong! This is terrible! This is blasphemy!' He was a very articulate man. My response was, 'John, let me ask you a question. I don't take the Scriptures literally. But I commend you and I applaud you, and I say God gave you the free will to take them literally. But Paul wrote in his letters to the Romans, as well as in his letter to the Corinthians, 'I shall not judge you, and you shall not judge me, for only God shall judge us both.' Even though *I* don't take the Scriptures literally, I'm not judging you. And you tell me you take them literally, and yet you're judging *me*! There's something wrong with that.' And there was silence. He didn't know what to say!" Nick laughed a laugh of delight that brought a smile to everyone's lips. It was not so much that he had managed to turn the tables on the fellow, but that he had managed to take the man's own words and show him he was living in contradiction. Nick wanted the whole world to know Jeshua's words in their hearts as well as their heads. Over the millennia, something happened where people's hearts had forgotten the beauty and simplicity of Jeshua's messages.

"God gave us free will," Nick continued, going after another bagel with cream cheese. "Whether it's the *Book of Revelation* or whatever, God gave us the free will to interpret it. There's two ways we can accept Scripture: We can accept it using our rational mind, our logic, or we can accept it through faith. And there are times when you may accept something that may not be logically right to you, but by faith you accept it. And other times you apply your logic. And sometimes you use both. That's the free will God gave to us. I don't accept the gloom, I don't accept those people who try to teach of God by putting fear into our hearts. I reject that kind of teaching. And I wish that other people would recognize that it's harmful, particularly to children, to have children growing up with fear in their hearts, wondering if God's going to punish them, wondering if this God they're learning about is going to send them to hell."

Georgie's eyes raised in grateful expectation. The afternoon session would be even better than she had guessed. Politely she let both men know it was time to get ready. Gary kidnapped one more chocolate chip cookie before going out the door. A crowd was already gathering around the front of the church.

The next day, Gary spent much of his time staring out his office window. After revealing to Brian all that had happened in Salem, he felt a kind of emptiness. Not the kind that leaves one with a sense of loss, but the other kind: the kind that feels as though all the burdens of the world have been washed away. He had heard similar comments from others after the Salem presentation. Nick had saved the last part of his session for what he called "The Healing of the Spirit." He had made sure to tell the congregation of his intentions, giving those who might be uncomfortable a chance to leave early. But none had left. All disposed themselves to an event that Nick, as Paul, had not exercised in 2,000 years. All who were there were affected in one way or another. Georgie had later called on the phone telling Nick, "For one thing, I awoke Monday morning, and got out of bed totally free of the body stiffness and discomfort I've been having for a year or so now. I believe this can be attributed to the spiritual healing you offered at the end of the afternoon session."

Gary replayed over and over again the sobbing of the lady who had sat three chairs down from him. Nick had come over to her after finishing his blessing of the assembly and held her in his arms. "Are you OK, dear?" he asked in the most gentle way. She was more than OK. She had somehow unleashed a torrent of guilt she had burdened herself with because of a divorce. She had given up her two children and a life that would have been intolerable. She had chosen a new life, but at the same time had cursed herself with untold guilt. She had never forgiven herself for relinquishing her children, or for rejecting her ex-husband. Nick's spiritual healing had included a section where the pains of divorce had been mentioned. He had encouraged those suffering from divorce, whether they were husband, wife, or children, to open themselves to a new kind of happiness, to forgive all who either injured or were injuring. Sometimes, our emotional wounds are far more serious than our physical wounds. And Gary had witnessed the consequence of letting go of such woundedness. In his heart, he knew that Nick was ready to face the world. He knew the time had arrived to test Nick's wings on a national level. But was the nation ready to hear? Only time would tell whether the many would be willing to move out of woundedness. Yes, indeed, sometimes we can be such a foolish people; we can be such a glorious people.

SIGN OF THE ANGELS

*T*o be completely truthful, Nick had not believed in angels. Like fairy godmothers and Easter bunnies, he thought them to be cute stories for the imaginations of children. It was not until they made their presence known to him personally that he understood the power of what is to come, and what he must do. The first time the angels spoke to Nick, they related, through a gifted woman named Sara, that they would make their presence known to him through the number 444. At the time, he dismissed this message as he had others. The number 4 had always been prominent in his life. It was his lucky number. Little did he know that the angels would not only make their presence known to him through this number but to thousands across the globe. After *The Messengers* had made known this sign of "444" from the angels, letters poured in from all over telling Nick how readers had felt the presence of angels in their lives.

One letter, in particular, arrived shortly after the release of the book. It was from a business professional, like Nick, and it had a particular impact on Nick at this time, as he began to realize he was not alone in being the object of angelic attention. The letter read:

Dear Nick,

I am writing this letter because I think, I believe, I need to talk to you. I will be as brief as I can. Yesterday, December 11, 1996, two things happened in my life. One I can understand, I lost my job with my company. The other, I cannot. It is the second incident that I need help with.

My youngest son plays hockey in Portland. Wednesday mornings he has practice at 5:30 a.m. Typically, he gets up and gets ready, then comes in and tells me it is time to leave. Since we only live 4 minutes from the rink, we usually do not leave earlier than necessary. Yesterday morning, I woke up before my son came in. I glanced at the clock and at 4:44 a.m. arose out of bed. My son and his two hockey friends were getting dressed. I went back to my room, got dressed, and told my son that I would wait for him in the car. I turned the car on, and the radio was set at 103.3 FM, a soft-rock station. But music was not playing. Instead, there was a man on the radio that told me to go out and buy the book, *The Messengers*, and that it would change my life.

I did not think much of it at that time. I went to my office in the morning knowing it was my last day there, and as I sat in my chair I was moved to get this book. I went to a local bookstore nearby but they did not have it. I called Powell's in Beaverton, and they had just sold their last one, but said I should contact the downtown store, which I did. They had a copy, and said they would hold it for me for up to three days. I usually am one to wait for the last minute to do things, but in this case I left the office immediately and purchased the book. I drove to our house in Beaverton.

I read "Chapter 1 — The Manuscript" and was in awe, yet confused. I knew that I had to get back to my office to get the news that I knew was coming. I got into my car and as I was driving, instead of going to my office, I was told to go tell my wife, Louise, what I just felt. Louise is a school teacher in Lake Oswego. I have driven to her school hundreds of times along the shore of Lake Oswego, and never thought of anything much. This time, I thought of you running (I am also a runner) and the leaves and needles under your shoes. As I was driving, I was looking at the lake and wondering where you had stopped. It was a very peaceful drive, even knowing that I had to go to my office afterwards.

I arrived at Louise's school and waited for her in her office in the gym. She knew what was happening at my office, so she thought that was why I was there. I surprised her with a smile on my face, and told her something happened to me today that I didn't understand, and that I was confused but felt at peace. I told her that I woke up at 4:44 in the morning and that it was significant, but to what degree, I was still not certain. I asked her to give me a little time to figure this out, and not to think that I was crazy.

I then proceeded to my office to receive the news I knew was coming (about losing my job), and it did not affect me the way I anticipated one day earlier. Three years ago, I was in a very serious accident. The doctor came into my room, looked at me, and said, 'John, you had an angel on your shoulder. You should be paralyzed, possibly even dead.' I just thought I was lucky!

My wife came home after work, and we sat in my office at home and discussed what happened with my job, but the conversation turned to what I was experiencing in my life. I tried to explain what was going on, showed her the book, explained the significance of 4:44 (that morning), and said I was still confused. That night we went to bed early and I brought the book with me to read (by the way I never read in bed). I read "Chapter 2 — the 444s," and when I got to [the part where the angels are having Rick Eckard write down information], my wife heard me exclaim, "Wow." What I was reacting to was what Rick had written at the bottom of the page: "Don't be afraid."

At one of the lowest points of my life, February 25, 1992, I was lying in a bed all alone and a very strong, soothing voice said to me, "John, don't be afraid." A couple of years later, I was sitting in a very small meeting with a group of people I did not know, and I shared this experience with them. A lady looked at me and said, "You are blessed. You must share this with others." I have not shared this experience with anyone else other than my wife, Louise, my daughter, Joanna, and now you.

This morning, December 12, 1996, I again woke up and saw 4:44 a.m. What I did not know until later in the morning was that Louise also woke up at exactly 4:44 a.m. I think this scared her.
It is about noon on the 12th, and I just finished "Chapter 3 — The Sound of Wings." I, too, twice in my life, have experienced the glow of golden lights from the sky I could not explain. I am not

sure why I am writing to you, other than maybe you can help make some sense of what is and has happened in my life, and these experiences that I have felt.

My life has been filled with hills and valleys, events that I now understand, some I am beginning to understand, and some that I still do not understand. If you have the time, I would love to just sit and talk with you.

Thank you for taking the time to read this. After reading only three chapters of *The Messengers*, I knew you would understand what has been locked inside of me for years. Merry Christmas!

> John G.

Nick read this letter with a sense of appreciation, and a sense of knowing. It was at this time that he began to realize that he was not alone in his journey. Hundreds, maybe thousands, now knew what he knew: Angels are here now to work with humankind. And when they come into your life, you want to believe with all your might that it is really happening, but maybe, just maybe, you're making the whole thing up. Maybe, just maybe, we shouldn't talk to anyone about any of this. Nick had not wanted to admit to himself that he was the return of the soul and spirit of Paul the Apostle. And in similar fashion, he had not wanted to admit that angels were talking to him when it first happened. Nick saw in John's letter the echoes of himself.

Five months later, Nick received another letter from John, a letter of confession. It would remind Nick how he must continue in his efforts to listen, to hear the divine as it works in our everyday lives.

May 15, 1997

Dear Nick:

In December of 1996, I wrote you a letter explaining how I first came in contact with your book, *The Messengers*, and what events have occurred in my life. When I first came in contact with your book, I was awakened several mornings at 4:44 a.m. When I started to read your book, I began to believe that I, too, had been "contacted" by my angel.

There were several times, while reading your book, when I was extremely moved by what I had read and how I was feeling at the moment. However, I got to chapter 11 and put the book down. In looking back, now, I think at that moment, I became afraid of what I was reading and getting myself into, and how I was feeling. I put the book away and did not pick it up again. Since that time, I have had no more contacts at 4:44 a.m. or p.m.

About a week ago, my wife asked me if I had ever finished reading your book, and I sheepishly said no. On Tuesday of this week, I got up and got ready to go to morning Mass. That morning, I happened to pick up my little Bible that I kept with me while I was incarcerated at Sheridan [a correctional facility]. In my Bible, I would write notes to myself almost like it was my spiritual diary. When I arrived at Mass that morning, I was kneeling and happened to open it to the back page. I almost fell over when I read what I had written. More specifically, when I had written it. The message I had written to myself started this way: "It is 4:44 p.m. on 10-25-90." The message I had written was about my relationship to God and Jesus. The time of this writing absolutely floored me! This was almost seven years before I had even heard of you or the book, The Messengers. I called my wife at her work and told her that I now have to finish reading your book. She said, "John, you won't believe this, but this morning I woke up at 4:44 a.m.!"

I now know that I have to finish reading your book. I am not sure how or what I will feel when I am done, but I will write to you and let you know.

Thanks!
John G.

John's letters told a common tale about us all. His was not a unique story; his struggle and self-discovery is a story that could be said of each one of us. Even when we try to deny the heavenly within our midst, it still is there trying to awaken us, help us, work with us. The reason why John's letters were among Nick's favorites was because of their sincerity, their truth, their honesty. John embodied the fear we all seem to carry with us when we realize that something is happening in our lives that we may not want, or do not understand. And the reason we don't want it stems from our inward terror of having to surrender notions with which we have grown too familiar, notions that have allowed us to settle for being less than who we are. Why is it easier to stare at our feet when we can look up and see the beauty reflected back to us in this mirror we call life?

Months after his letters had been sent, John came to a place of strange peace. Upon reflection, he realized how even his worst moments had provided him with important lessons. At one point he had owned a $5 million-a-year company ... and lost it. He had almost lost his family after finding himself incarcerated in minimum security at Sheridan. But something kept speaking to his soul, kept showing him where he might find his true happiness. And in the end, that happiness was found. With a pleasant smile and eyes that pierced one's soul, John frankly confessed that he did not have abundance after losing his job and finding another. But he frankly confessed that he was now the happiest he had ever been. And it was reflected in his family. When asked what message he would give to the world if given the opportunity, he responded without hesitation, "Open your hearts. Open your ears. Open your eyes. Don't be afraid." John had found peace with himself ... with a little help from his "friends."

It was around this time that Nick was receiving more and more information from the angels. Sleep was almost impossible to come by at times. So much change was entering his own life that he would arrive at the corporate offices yearning to read the letters now arriving from around the world, telling him how others were also facing change. His communication with the angels was becoming stronger, clearer, and more descriptive as they began to provide more information about the changes that would transform the entire world. These were not changes that would bring doom and destruction, but changes that would flood humanity with realizations, new wonder, new ways of perceiving ourselves and our planet. Had not the angels told Nick that 444 represented the power of God's love, letting us know the angels are there for us, that 444 was to become the symbol for thousands of people, perhaps someday millions? Had not the angels increasingly opened channels of communication to those who would simply allow it?

The following letter not only echoes the fear John faced, it also demonstrates a common theme heard repeatedly in letter after letter delivered to Nick's offices. Many others attest through their letters to the puzzling guilt we carry around that tends to force us to make the unwarranted assumption that humankind is basically sinful, or evil. The angels tell us that nothing is further from the truth. God is within each one of us. We are vessels of light, a light that is a part of God. The only evil that exists is the evil we choose to create. It is not authored by God. Consider the kind of world we would inhabit if we all chose to see the inherent goodness that dwells within each of us. Would a criminal choose to rob a store if he felt loved, and in turn loved? If those around him had treated him with compassion, and had spoken with the kind of truth that opens any heart, no matter how hardened, would he not have been able to address his needs — whether material, emotional, or spiritual? Would not his fears, his inner darkness be confronted by a light that already resides within? Listen as one person tells the rest of us how we change one single life, and ultimately the world.

Dear Mr. Bunick,

I don't know where exactly to start. I just feel it's time I try and find out more information. I am so grateful for your appearance on [the TV show] "Northwest Afternoon" in Seattle a few weeks ago. It, in some way, gave me a partial answer to what's been going on in my life since 1992.

It wasn't until that day when you were on "Northwest Afternoon" that I first had any suspicion that something could be happening of an angelic nature. I had just sat down for a moment with my 14-year-old daughter and her friend, just to find out about their day and relax for a couple of minutes. We turned the TV on only half-listening, but being drawn more and more by the conversation. We were frustrated that [the host] never let you finish any sentence to a question she asked you. Frankly, your story was compelling but I wanted to allow for ... well ... could this man be a fruitcake like half of the televangelists we hear so much about?

Then the host asked you about the significance of 444. I felt a rush, and my daughter leaped off the sofa yelling at me, "Mom, are you listening?" Until then, I chalked it all up to coincidence.

I worked for QFC, a local grocery store, while we built our dream home. Something started happening a few months after I became a cashier. The number 444, or 4.44 would come up on the cash register. So much so, that I asked the other cashiers. They thought I was crazy, and, after a while, told me I should play the Lotto. They were my lucky numbers. Not only was it happening at work but many times I'd look at the clock and it would say 4:44. I, never in a million years, could imagine what it was. I never felt any evil. I just thought I'm somehow locked into 444 for whatever reason.

You can imagine the feelings that came over me when I heard you talk about 444s and the angels. I've always kind of felt God didn't like me, and was determined to make my life challenging until I go crazy. I had myself convinced that I just never give enough to others, or don't believe enough, or I am not a good enough person to be able to have a peaceful life. I feel *differently* now.

Anyway, I had gone to the bookstore a few weeks ago to find a book for some business associates. I had very little time, but as I was racing down the aisles, I was stopped in my tracks by a book that caught my eye, and I felt compelled to reach for it. I turned it over to find it was your book. I dropped everything and looked for anything on 444. I sat right there and read that entire chapter. I bought the book and had a very hard time putting it down.

Every free moment I had, I had to read. I felt like I was there living it with you. I had the most peaceful yet euphoric feelings as I read the book. I never wanted it to end. I still need more.

When I was through with the book, I started thinking it's just a coincidence about my 444s, and I've never felt I had a message, and the best to my knowledge I had never been awakened at 4:44 a.m. ... until about 1 1/2 weeks ago — the day before I left on my trip to California for work reasons, and to see friends and family. I am currently on a plane going home this minute.

Anyway, I remember hearing a popping noise in my room. It's kind of a familiar noise. Our house cracks at night sometimes. It woke me out of a very sound sleep, but I went back to sleep realizing it was the house popping. However, it continued to pop and crack over and over and over until something told me to wake up all the way and look at the clock. It was 4:44 a.m., and my heart jumped out of my chest and started racing. When I realized what could be happening, I laid on my back trying to calm down, and told myself, listen … listen … listen. All I heard was dead silence. I laid there for 25 minutes and I realized the house didn't make one more sound.

I told my family about it. My husband said to me, "What is it going to take to get you to find out what's going on?" I guess that's why I am writing you. I keep thinking this is all made up and it's a coincidence. There is nothing about me that angels would want, but I still find myself bothered and wondering. I would really like to talk to your angel lady and find out once and for all so I can put this thing to rest or know for sure what's going on.

Can you help me? Please contact me — please don't think I'm crazy. You must be getting all kinds of letters or phone calls like mine of people assuming they are in the presence of something extraordinary.

I have never witnessed a miracle of birds on a lake or heard wings or wrote messages. So, I kind of think I'm a fruitcake, too!
I just need to know what, if anything is going on. Thank you, and thank you for your book.

Kathie

Nick was touched by the sincerity of Kathleen's letter. It deserved a personal response. Taking his Dictaphone in hand, he spoke from his heart about the importance of seeing how important each one of us is. "God is here for you," he said intently. Many of us think we are unworthy, when the exact opposite is true. The earth itself depends on our knowing and believing that God is within each one of us. "We need to accept that," he affirmed. If every single person believes in their importance with God, and in God, then each of us will ultimately change the world. The occurrences of 444 experiences has manifold purposes. But chief among them is being reminded that the angels are here for us. They wish us to acknowledge them, and in so doing, enlist their aid and comfort. For there is little they can do without our asking it of them. The 444 experiences are reminders and indicators that the angelic realm is trying to work with us.

Kathleen usually did not write letters — in fact she never writes letters. But upon reading Nick's response, she thanked herself for her own courage. And from that day on, courage became her watchword and her byword. In fact she made a copy of Nick's credo, found in the last pages of chapter seven of *The Messengers*, framed it and hung it on her wall. Particularly noted is the following section:

> You must believe in yourself at all times. You must never lose faith that you are capable of doing anything in life you choose to do. And you must always choose the highest. It is not enough for you to choose that you must achieve excellence. For you must believe in yourself enough to accomplish that which others cannot accomplish.
>
> To believe in yourself, you must have courage that exceeds the need for consideration of courage. It must be a natural part of your life that avoids any need for decision-making based on whether you have courage to do that which you must. This must be a belief beyond personal question, beyond personal doubt, to a point when it can no longer be considered courage, but a way of life. This shall be so, for you will believe in yourself.

Kathleen's journey was no longer one in which she thought that God could not, did not, love her. Hers was now a journey of courage, self-courage. It is that kind of singular courage that moves into the collective whole of society, touches it, speaks softly to it, and forever changes it. Kathleen's newfound courage made her a beacon of love and acceptance, for she now was able to love and accept the gift she, herself, was in this world. The angels had opened her eyes to the truth of who she was. Truly, this kind of self-discovery is the key that, when turned, unlocks the treasure that is ours. Imagine a world of people who see their own inherent goodness, believe in it, and live it. How can such reality not change this world forever? We have only to look at Kathleen to believe in its possibility.

Wherever Nick would go, whether in restaurants or airports, people began to approach him telling about 444 experiences they had witnessed and/or experienced. It amazed even him to hear how varied and numerous the stories were. As coming events approach, it becomes increasingly obvious that the angels are seeking a communion with the people of the Earth. One night, Nick decided to ask the angels why there were so many reports of the 444 phenomenon. And they answered back to him, "It is because we have always been here, but only now do the people of the Earth ask us to help them. We have been waiting."

PART II

A TIME FOR HEALING

5

THE SECRET

M ad Dog, why don't you have Julia Ingram regress you to find out how much you can add to all that's been uncovered?" Nick had hinted around before at revealing Gary's ancient past but this was the first time he'd been so blunt.

Taking a sip of pinot noir, Gary let silence linger for a while longer. "I have my reasons," he mumbled. With his fingers steadily rotating the stem of the wineglass, his eyes stared trancelike into the rich redness, thinking what a treat these dinners were. Like Solomon, Nick had an appreciation for good food and good wine. Had not Solomon proclaimed these two blessings the only worthwhile pursuits of life? Everything else was folly?

"Oh come on, Mad Dog. You know more about me than even my kids." Which was saying something, considering how few really knew Nick at all. Nick valued his privacy as much as he did his business investments.

"I don't know, Nick," still turning the stem of the wineglass. "I've been regressed before, and promised myself I wouldn't allow it to happen again."

Nick smiled. He loved a challenge. "That bad?"

"Not really. What happened is beyond believing. I can still hardly believe it myself. How can I expect anyone else to take me seriously?"

Nick leaned forward, breaching etiquette by firmly placing his elbows on the table. "After all I've been through, you expect me to be less open-minded than you've been with me?" As he finished the sentence, Nick reached for the wine bottle and began refilling both glasses. For Gary, Oregon pinot noir was nectar of the gods. *Wasn't this supposed to be a business planning dinner?* Gary asked to himself. Nick's insatiable curiosity stood as a force to be reckoned with. The man knew how to get what he wanted. And how did the old adage go — "The truth is in the wine"? Can insatiable curiosity be justified in pursuit of the truth?

"It's not so much about being open-minded," Gary countered gently. "Don't you think some things are better left alone? Some mysteries should just remain a mystery?" Gary ceased playing with his wine glass and looked straight into Nick's eyes, trying to catch a glimpse into Nick's soul.

"Normally, Mad Dog, I might agree with you. But who knows what's ahead for both of us? Life is too short. We are at the dawning of great mysteries being revealed. And who knows what you have hidden away? It may contain an important piece to the jigsaw puzzle we are trying to figure out. Besides, you know I can keep a secret. And you look like you need to get this off your chest." Nick was right. He could keep a secret — when he wanted to. The real question was whether he wanted to.

Gary removed his spectacles and massaged his eyes, letting out a sigh. "It all started in 1983 when I came down with what would be diagnosed as an incurable disease." Nick leaned back on his chair letting the restaurant chatter surrounding them fade away. This was going to be better than he'd thought.

"What kind of disease?"

"Well, no one knew at first. Later it was diagnosed by a well-known dermapathologist as subdermal-something-or-other-something-or-other. All I know is that it was like being cursed with poison ivy, only all the time. Really awful stuff. Started one day after picking Gravenstein apples all afternoon in the hot sun. Got bark dust all over me trying to get the last apple from the tree top.

Gravensteins make the absolute best applesauce. I went back home with my booty and crashed on the couch. When I woke up and stripped to take a shower, I started noticing a rash. When I stepped out of the shower, the rash seemed to be all over me but I dismissed it as my skin reacting to the hot shower. By midnight the rash had erupted into hives, accenting any crease or crack where the bark dust had been. I looked like a drawing done in red ink, itching all over — unbearable. Had to go to the hospital because there was no way I could sleep. The emergency room doctors put me on prednisone and Demoral. Told me to soak in the tub at home until the itching stopped. For seventy-two hours I lay in the tub soaking in oat water. Couldn't eat, couldn't sleep. After I finally left the tub, tiny blisters broke out in every imaginable crack and crevice of my body. The itching finally lessened, but now orange ooze started to cover me as the blisters broke. The ooze hardened into orange plastic-looking scabs. Thought I should tell this part before dinner arrived." Taking another sip of the wine, Gary stole a glance at Nick to see how squeamish he looked.

"Nice of you to tell me now," Nick kidded, noticing the waiter coming with their salads. "No problem; go on." Gary decided to wait until the waiter finished with the plates, taking note of the matador-like fashion in which he placed the first course, as if a cape were being laid before them instead of plates of baby bib lettuce.

After waving off the peppercorn grinder, Gary continued, "With the orange plastic scabs covering me, I looked like something out of a Star Trek movie. I couldn't work in that condition. If I so much as bent my arms to type on my computer, the scabs would crack like thin peanut brittle and let out ooze all over again. I couldn't even leave the house. My wife spent as much time with me as possible, but someone had to work."

"You were married?"

"We're coming to that part. After six months of scabbing and healing, oozing and scabbing, with the whole cycle repeating over and over again, including episodic visits to the emergency room, I lost my job. Which meant I also lost my house, lost my self-respect, and almost lost my wife. For a year I saw every doctor, every specialist, every allergist I could think of. But to no avail.

"The second year, I resorted to alternative medicine, seeing acupuncturists, homeopaths, herbologists, even shamans — you name it, I saw it. Nothing worked. Since I couldn't get a job, I began doing computer consulting and started my own digital music company. At the time MIDI had just hit the market. Even though I couldn't read a note of music, I could generate copy by paying musicians to keyboard in the notes and then I'd clean it up later. I understood the mathematics of music and had no trouble creating publishing quality songbooks and sheet music at a quarter of the price of the old way. Because of the efficiency and reliability of the technology, I managed to snag a lucrative contract with a major publishing house. That was my baptism into publishing and writing. And it allowed me to remain a recluse, since the disease continued reinfecting me into the third year. By that time, I discovered how to reduce the reoccurrence of infections by having my wife pressure cook all my underwear. Even if one drop of residue serum were left anywhere on my cleaned clothes, the rash would start all over again. Can you imagine having to pressure cook your clothes? Because of this discovery, I could actually start to act normal again, going for a couple of weeks or more at a time without another bout of infection."

Gary picked at his salad. The memory of the agony he had gone through took his appetite away. Nick's salad languished as well. He was too enthralled with what he was hearing. "So, you gave up on modern medicine; you gave up on alternative medicine. What was left?"

A smile fought away the blushing on Gary's face as he pondered how to answer the question. "I began reading everything I could on the unexplainable: *Life After Death*, *Life After Life*, *To Hear the Angels Sing*, and finally Dr. Brian Weiss' book, *Many Lives, Many Masters*. That book changed my life. Weiss originally started out to debunk what was then being called 'The New Psychology,' which included past-life regression hypnosis. But instead of debunking it, he ended up becoming one of its strongest proponents. In the book, he had a patient whose case was as hopeless as mine. Wild stuff. I decided I'd have to find someone like Brian Weiss. And you know me. When I put my mind to something, neither heaven nor earth can stop me."

The salad plates disappeared as the waiter readied the table for the main course. Nick wished the waiter would disappear but waited patiently for what he knew would be a culinary marvel. The two men were pampering themselves in one of Nick's favorite restaurants, hidden away in Northwest Portland. Being hidden away had done little good in the way of coziness, for the reputation of the chef had spread throughout the city as well as the suburbs. Getting a reservation could prove difficult at times. But Nick made it a point to be remembered. His generosity served him well at times like this. For "Mr. Bunick," a table could always be found, accompanied by great wine and a great feast. As the last of the main course was set, Nick returned to the conversation. "Had you heard about Julia at this time?"

"This was just before Julia got a name for herself. Finding a therapist well versed in classical psychotherapy, like Weiss, was daunting. I wasn't having much luck. But one night, while watching the Community Cable Channel, I stumbled on a trance channeler. Well, kind of a trance channeler. He wasn't like J.Z. Knight. He could move in and out of his trance at will, carrying on a cogent conversation with you when he wasn't channeling information. He brought through an entity he called 'Maitreya.' I couldn't take my eyes off what I was seeing. Callers were phoning in with outrageous questions, only to get the most incredible answers. I decided to try and call in, and actually got through. Being the skeptic I am, I wanted to ask him a question he couldn't possibly know or guess the answer to. It was a question about the *bardo*, or afterlife. Did I get the surprise of my life when he stated over the air that I had already died when I was a child, and had been sent back to bring new information to the world. There was no way he could have even guessed at that. But it was true. I had drowned in a river during a family reunion when I was eleven, and had been pronounced dead. Through all my years, I'd never told anyone what happened to me as my body lay on the bottom of that river. I had gone to a place I call the 'God-Light,' where love is beyond description — sheer ecstasy. When I had been told by the God-Light that I had to return, I objected vociferously. But even before finishing my sentence, I found myself back in my body. The rescuers had found me by then, and had covered my body in an army blanket, ready to cart it off. They didn't have mouth-to-mouth resuscitation in those days. I remember being so utterly confused under the blanket by all the weeping and wailing I could hear. How could anybody be sad with all this love pouring in? When my body started to move, pulling the blanket back, you should have heard the screaming. My parents never spoke about that afterwards.

"So you can understand why I was a bit stunned that this channeler knew such information. After the TV show, I decided to make an appointment with him. It was during my private session with him when he told me, 'On December 15th you will experience a heavenly event which will affect you and everyone around you.' This was in March when he told me this. Plus, he told me I would be moving to Seattle. I laughed on my way out the door. There was no way I was moving to Seattle. I had this big publishing contract, and there was no way I would walk away from that. Hah! A few months later, deeper into the contractual obligations, I realized Portland didn't have large enough of a talent pool to finish the work that needed to be done on the songbooks and a hymnal. So guess where I moved? Yep. Seattle."

The waiter now moved in between the tables with ballerina grace. The matador must have gone on vacation. Water glasses were filled and wine goblets carefully topped. The gracefulness and efficiency caught Gary off guard. For the first time that evening, he focused on someone other than himself. Even the waiter's eyes danced. Noticing the pinot noir bottle empty, he asked if another bottle would be desired. Nick looked to Gary. "Why not?" Gary answered with bravado, "I think I'll need it." Nick wondered what he meant but decided not to ask. The evening was unfolding beautifully. Why interrupt the flow? Business affairs would surrender to another time.

As Gary finally dove into his dinner, his mind worked at how to reveal to Nick the real pearl of this story. "As December approached, the skin condition grew worse. I heard about a famous derma-pathologist at the University of Washington who might be able to help me. Normally it took one to two years to get an appointment with him. When I phoned in, someone had just canceled. Ya gotta love such coincidences. Three days later I was sitting in his office. For the rest of the month, the more he worked on me the worse I got. When he finally told me that what I had was incurable, that I'd have it the rest of my life, I was furious. I was furious with him and his profession, and I was furious with God. I felt like Job in the *Bible*. Completely abandoned. Cursed with a dreaded skin disease that would torment me to my dying day. The specialist gave me prescriptions like all the rest had done. He told me I could have a normal life if I continued to use hydrocortisone. Doctors must think people are stupid. I'd already done my research and knew the consequences of continued use of such steroids. I left the office fuming all the way down to my car. I had made a promise to myself that if it ever came to getting such a life-sentence, I'd do whatever I could to find someone who knew about the New Psychology."

"So you found someone to regress you?" Nick asked trying to push the story along.

"Not just someone, but someone who knew both classical psychotherapy and past-life regression. Took me a while, but I found just the man in Bellevue, Washington — a wonderful doctor of psychology, named Dr. Larry DeHerrera. It wasn't easy for me to call him, since I didn't know what exactly I was getting myself in for. When he answered the phone, I asked him about his credentials and he asked me questions about my case. When we finished interrogating one another, he told me that he wasn't accepting any more clients, that he was full up. However, my case was so intriguing, he decided he would slide me into the one remaining slot he reserved for his usual patients, in case of an emergency. When I asked him the date and time, he told me December 15th. I sat there stunned, and then mumbled 'Holy shit.' He asked me if there was something wrong, and I told him that everything was just fine, the date would be just fine. Hah. If I had only known. The channeler had been correct. This date would end up changing my entire life." Silence hung in the air while Gary nibbled at his dinner. Telling this story always brought back old feelings of anxiety. Before he laid into the most difficult part of the story, Gary listened to conversations going on around him. He'd always been blessed with exceptional hearing, and eavesdropping had been a curious pastime for him.

From past experience he'd learned that the more conversations going on around him meant the less likely his conversation would be sat in on. All the adjacent tables were engaged in serious chat. He would proceed with his tale.

"The first session, Dr. DeHerrera tried to use hypnosis to get at the source of my incurable disease. Nothing happened. So the next couple of sessions were spent with classical psychotherapy. Which made me glad I had taken the time to find someone of his talent. In the middle of one of the therapy sessions, Doc, as he encouraged me to call him, said, 'Ya know, Gary, you are really a good psychologist.' I laughed thinking he was making jest. 'No,' he continued, 'I'm serious. You really know your stuff. It's obvious you are well read on the topic. I'm truly impressed. But I tell you what. Why don't you give it a rest? Let me be the psychologist. You're paying me good money to help you. Why not just relax and let me work with you.' Wow, did that catch me by surprise. And frankly, it wasn't easy to do what he asked. Doc was teaching me a lot about myself. It was the next session where he really threw me for a loop. With those kind eyes of his, he stared right through me and said, 'Hrumph, you remind me of me. I'd like to tell you a story about me. I used to really feel lonely much of the time. It wasn't because I hadn't any friends. I had many, but they weren't there when I truly needed them. And that puzzled me. I realized that life is like a canvas. Each of us tries to paint our lives, our souls, on the canvas. And right next to us our friends are painting on their canvases as well. I discovered that my friends used to love to look at my canvas. I think it is the same for you. Here I am painting away, showing my love and my life to my friends as I paint. But when I look over at their canvases, they have stopped painting. They are standing there looking at mine. And that's when I felt the most lonely. I wanted to see their paintings but there was nothing more to see. Ya know what I discovered, Gary? Sometimes you have to put your fuckin' brush down ... so you don't feel such loneliness even among friends.' Nick, that guy took my breath away at times. I couldn't talk for about ten minutes after that, I was so choked up. He had me nailed.

"About the second week of January, Doc looked at me and said point blank, 'We are done. There is nothing wrong with you psychologically.' That one rattled me royally. 'What do you mean we're done,' I protested. 'You haven't done all you can do.' And he looked at me with one of those sagelike looks of his and asked, 'And what more would you have me do?' Damn, could he ever turn the tables on me. I practically yelled at him, 'You haven't even attempted the hypnosis again. And why not? That's the main reason why I came here.' And he retorted, 'That's what I was waiting to hear. Shall we begin?' "

Nick had to grin at such candor and cleverness. As he waited for Gary to continue the story, he knew that some long-held secret would was about to be uncloaked. It was time to fill Gary's wineglass again. As he leaned over with the bottle, Gary laid his hand across the top of the goblet. "No thanks. I need to have a clear head to tell the rest of this."

"Tell me this," Nick said. "Why do you think the therapist spent so much time with classical psychotherapy when he knew you were there for this new stuff?"

"I think he truly understood that I had gotten in my own way, that I was still getting in my own way in doing what I came here to do. We had discussions about what it was I would be looking for while under hypnosis. Was it more than finding the cause of the disease? And it turns out that I did want to know more than the cause of the disease. I read volumes on the possibilities available using past-life regression. And one of the areas most interesting to me takes place in what is called the *bardo*. This is the realm of the afterlife. The Tibetans believed in eight *bardos*. However, modern regression work had only explored two: life after death and life before life. Raymond Moody had done breakthrough work in that arena and others followed suit. I wanted to know why I was sent here. In one of our sessions, Doc found out about my having died in the drowning accident. He wanted to know what had been said while I was on the other side. So the both of us were interested in finding out why I had been sent back. Who was I? What was I sent here to do? We didn't know if we would be allowed to find the answers to these questions but both of us were quite interested in uncovering that part of the painting that was my life."

"So what happened?"

Nick was all ears as Gary began to describe the session, describing how the hypnosis finally took, how Doc had simply asked one short sentence once Gary was under: "Let us find the cause of this disease." That was it. This simple request called forth swirling scenes wrapped within the other. Each scene laid out a lifetime of confrontation and enlightenment with the status quo throughout history. Doc asked for detail from each passing scene, hoping to find out as much as possible that would give the underlying cause of the disease. But before much detail could be discerned, another lifetime would roll in on top of the other. It was as if these lives were being lived concurrently. But that wasn't possible, was it? How could one life be lived in colonial America, while another was being lived in ancient Egypt? The rolling scenes settled into one particular lifetime in 17th century France. Gary had been a famous cathedral architect. Nick noted each piece of detail as Gary described how he had fashioned a statement into one of the cathedrals, which was not uncommon for architects to do at that time, especially architects with a large following. The architect had under him many apprentices, who in turn not only mastered his mathematical techniques but also adopted his sense of justice and righteousness for the downtrodden.

Gary looked up at Nick to check whether he should divulge the next piece of information. He decided he would. The architect had fallen in love with the Lord Mayor's daughter. They were engaged to be married. Their love for one another surpassed any found in stories or lore — for both fully adored the gifts of the other, the richness of life they both brought one another. The supreme irony of this love lay in the architecture of the newly finished cathedral. For the architect had been an outspoken critic of conservative elements within the Catholic Church, and how they had taken love and sexuality out of its sacredness, focusing instead on any and every aspect considered sinful. This Baroque period had been a period of religious fervor and spiritual revolution. How could love ever be sinful? These conservative voices within the Catholic Church threw a dark shadow on the splendor of love in a time of enlightenment, and the architect wished to make a statement against them.

Elements of the new cathedral reflected conservative echoes of Renaissance architecture in its rectangular and circular shapes, as well as Gothic architecture in the use of downspouts, not unlike the conservative elements within the changing Church. High atop the cathedral roofing stood rows of gargoyle-like angels ready to carry any excessive water away from the walls of the beautiful structure. The building was lauded as an architectural marvel by the bishop and the city elders. But what they didn't know showed itself one stormy night. An evening thunderstorm dropped buckets of water on the city, giving way to parting clouds undraping a full moon. The downspouts proved their worthiness, sending out copious streams off the cathedral roof. But what the architect had not accounted for was a full moon silhouetting the gargoyles, betraying his clever secret. From ground level, the angelic beings no longer looked so angelic. In fact, the entire cathedral appeared lined with a row of large penises taking a collective whiz off the cathedral roof. The wings of the angels no longer appeared so winglike but more like matching scrota to the phallic angels the architect had humorously designed. The sight was not lost on the townsfolk. A crowd gathered — some in shock, others in hysterical laughter. The subtle statement no longer served to be so subtle. Word spread like a plague. When the bishop heard of the incident days later, the Lord Mayor and the town elders found themselves in the bishop's quarters. How dare such scandal come to the diocese and the city. Something had to be done. The first step was to summon the architect, remove any and all support for his school and his followers, issue an edict of shame, and ostracize him before the entire city.

Rather than fight the establishment and rally his supporters, the architect found himself devastated, abandoned by his bride-to-be, sent away by her farther. The engagement had been immediately canceled, with any talk of a marriage completely out of the question. The architecture's apprentices wanted to rally the voices of architectural freedom, hoping to take advantage of the creative fervor of the age. But the Church fathers threatened a heavy hand on any who dared show any form of support for this outrageous scandal. The cathedral now had been facetiously dubbed the Cathedral of the Night Waters, forcing the bishop to enlist renovations of the gargoyles as quickly as masons could be found.

Instead of becoming a rebel for free architectural expression, for the city as well as the whole of France, the architect took to drink, becoming instead the town drunk. His fall was quick and total. One night, while in a drunken stupor, he rode out of the city on a road that skirted a church graveyard. Not paying attention to the trees along the road, he clotheslined himself with a sagging tree limb, falling from his horse into a ravine, breaking his neck in the process. As he lay dying in the ravine, townsfolk found him in the early morning. Because the neck fracture had paralyzed him, he was thought dead. And because he had been ostracized, the local priest made it known that he could not be buried in any cemetery. A small crew assembled to cover the body with dirt where it lay. And as the shoveled dirt piled upon the architect, he had no choice but to watch himself being buried alive.

"Alive?" Nick broke in. "You watched yourself being buried alive?" Nick remembered the vividness of his own regression sessions with Julia Ingram, especially the beating of the Apostle Paul. So real had been the scene that bruises had appeared on his arms. The thought of watching oneself being buried alive ran through his body with a shudder.

"Well, yeah, I watched the first several shovelsful. Doc quickly took me beyond the death and into the *bardo*, not wanting me to suffer any longer. Then he asked me what the scene around me looked like, what it felt like. I told him that there was nothing but peace, which was so amazing, since I had freshly experienced the panic of being buried alive. The peace was beyond description, kind of like the passage in Scripture: '... peace that passes understanding.' Gold light surrounded me, no matter where I looked. Love filled the gold light, which filled me with this rich sense of profound peace. Fantastic experience. I'll never forget it.

"Then Doc asked what was my mission in coming here to Earth at this time, as we had agreed early on. It was then that an angelic being appeared in front of me a distance away. At least, I thought it was an angel. Never in my born days have I seen anything like it. In place of a face there shone this featureless countenance, lustrous with an incredible white light. Its body seemed made of half substance and half light, maybe eight to ten feet high. The top half, from its left shoulder down to its right hip, looked as though it were made of prisms within prisms, rainbows within rainbows of glowing light. The most vivid colors imaginable. I remember thinking whatever this was looked like a Picasso painting, only alive. The being's lower half sported a robelike garment shining with iridescence, as if it were made of mother of pearl. The outline around the apparition diffused into a soft mist which emitted constant love. Then the angel began to speak. And when it spoke, I could hear it on three different levels simultaneously. In my mind it issued what I would call a holographic message while a spoken message came through my own voice. The holographic message was like having an encyclopedia stuffed into your brain, enabling you to know all the knowledge contained there all at once. As soon as I would have a single thought, the holographic knowledge would explode into fragments and turn into what could be described as separate books on a library shelf. Any of these books could be visited later for their content and knowledge. And while this was going on, I could feel a subconscious message moving into my heart. As all this unfolded, I could also see my conscious self sitting to the side wondering what in the hell was happening. My conscious self sat there like a cougar ready to jump in if this got any more weird or if something didn't seem right. My conscious self knew that it could end this whole session in a split second if it wanted.

"The angel gave the answer to Doc's inquiry through my voice, saying, "Your purpose is the same now as it has always been: To bring justice to the unjust, to lift up the downtrodden, to throw light into the shadows created by man's efforts to make evil out that which holds beauty and harmony. It is the same in this lifetime as it has been in every lifetime." I don't think Doc had a clue that the angel had appeared or knew where this message had come from.

"What Doc didn't hear was the holographic message, the encyclopedia in my brain. This volume of information allowed me to see all my pertinent lifetimes in full concert and harmony with regards to this spoken message. Seeing this composite allowed me to realize how I existed in more ways than I thought. There are those who come to Earth as more than simple human beings. Multi-dimensions exist, and to those who live in those composite dimensions, they bear a holographic soul. I had entered the Earth time and time again to set forth new truths, justice, and righteousness. Powers that I did not understand or realize with my conscious mind could be given to humanity, or humanity could be made to remember its past abilities with these incomprehensible gifts. I had come once again in this lifetime to bring gifts and to address matters of injustice. The holographic message was so pervasive that an entire book would have to be written to explain all the wrongs that had been created and perpetrated in the name of stamping out the 'evil' of homosexuality. When in reality, homosexuality is nothing more than a remedy to man's creation of separateness, having divided his masculine and feminine, putting them at war with one another. In separating masculine from feminine, man needed a bridge back to oneness, oneness with himself and also with the God-Light. That bridge was the holding together of the masculine and feminine in one, a witness to the original time spoken of in Genesis: 'And God created Man. Male and female he created them, and he blessed them and named them Man when they were created.' In the English translation, it is made to sound like God created men and then he created women. But in the original Hebrew, especially in sections of the Zohar, we realize that Man was both male and female in the same body. This same truth is reflected in the name of God. In English, God is male. But in Hebrew the word for God, Yahweh, is neuter. Not the English neuter, which means neither male or female, but the Hebrew neuter, which means both male and female. In our modern world, Carl Jung, the great psychologist, discovered this same phenomenon in his writings on the *animus* and *anima*.

"Yet man has chosen to call that which is not masculine or feminine, but in reality both masculine and feminine, as sinful, so that mankind might destroy it. And in destroying it, humanity would not have to face the truth of how ego has separated us from God, separated us in our world, separated us from our inner selves. There is more, much more. It is all so intricately tied together."

Gary looked over at Nick to discern whether he had told too much. Nick scratched his chin sagaciously. "So do you still have access to all this information?"

"Well, let me finish my tale before I answer that. It may have an impact on the work we do together."

"Would either of you care for dessert?" the waiter asked, catching Gary by surprise. He'd been so absorbed in his storytelling that he'd phased out the entire restaurant.

"Actually, I could use some dessert," Gary volunteered. After ordering a large raspberry cobbler a la mode, he looked over at Nick, who waved off any further calories. As the waiter carried off the dessert menus, Gary took in a deep breath as he continued his bizarre account. He knew Nick was rapt by the story by the mere fact that he had not interrupted with his typical bombardment of questions.

"Then Doc asked if there was another mission. Before me appeared the other mission. I could tell that this mission contained a far greater purpose for me, and ramifications for others. The purpose appeared behind a scrim in the abstract shape of a shining ball, like a great pearl. The veil or scrim, as thin at as it was, acted to block any information coming forth from the pearl about this other purpose. Not sure what should be done, I told Doc, 'The purpose is hidden behind a curtain.' His response was, "Then let us draw the curtain back so that we may learn of this other purpose.' As I reached with my mind to draw the scrim back, the angel stepped in front of the curtain. It would not let the curtain be drawn. Again, not knowing what to do, I reported to Doc, 'I can't draw the curtain back. The angel won't let me. I can no longer see the purpose.' Doc's response came immediately. 'Angel?' His voice betrayed his wondering what the hell was going on. After a pause he added, 'Ask the angel to step aside so that we might know this other mission you came here with.' And the angel responded, once again using my voice, 'You may not know this at this time. For if you did, you might misuse it or abuse it.' For reasons I can't explain, I knew what the angel meant. Because of my own self-doubts I was not ready to know why I had truly come to the Earth, nor was I ready to handle the extraordinary gifts that were to be given to humanity."

Nick's curiosity got the better of him: "Do you know what the purpose and the gifts are now? Didn't this happen a couple of years ago?"

"Yes. I believe the mission has to do with the work you are trying to do with the Great Tomorrow, this marvelous organization you are trying to create. What my role is remains to be seen. And I believe the gifts have long been spoken of throughout history through prophecy from many religious traditions. At this point, I'm not exactly aware of what the gifts are."

"Don't you think a hypnosis session with Julia might bring some of this info forward?"

"Wait until you hear the rest of the story before I answer that." Dessert arrived. Gary toyed with the topping trying to reorganize his thoughts. Nick caught the eye of a business associate entering the restaurant. She waved, and then approached the table. Gary smiled and looked down at his dessert. He wondered how much he should tell Nick. This next part was going to be the toughest to tell. Nick politely made introductions, the associate's eyes wondering what kind of power dinner was unfolding. Business executives have a knack for picking up nonverbal clues or body language. Anyone who knew Nick knew how much he loved food. The fact that the dinner table was empty of everything but a raspberry cobbler and wineglasses told the associate that whatever was being discussed must be important. And since Nick imparted only polite chatter, the executive figured out she needed to leave the two men to their meeting.

Nick returned to Gary, "OK, where were we?"

"Well, when Doc heard that the angel would not let us see any more, he decided to end the session right then and there. My conscious mind, still sitting on the sideline was screaming, 'No, no, you can't. We have to find out why this angel is here. Don't stop now.' As Doc began to prepare me for leaving the *bardo*, my conscious mind stepped in saying aloud, 'You don't need to bring me out of this. I can bring myself out now.' I think my conscious mind was hoping to control what was happening and wanted to wrestle away Doc's ability to end it. But Doc insisted, 'Please let me do this. Just relax and let me guide you back. As I count backwards from ten to one ....' My conscious mind was not pleased as I came out of the hypnosis. In fact, I was pissed. What Doc was not aware of was that the angel gave me another message. Instead of giving the message on three levels at once, it began giving me the holographic message first. Another encyclopedia of information exploded into my brain. I can't tell you what a wild sensation this was. I kept wanting it never to go away but as soon as I had a single thought the hologram of knowledge would fracture into pieces and separate into fragments of knowledge."

"Can you give the overall sense of this holographic message? Or is that impossible with language?"

"The message told me of the wonder of my intentions to undo the sorrows that mankind had brought upon itself with sexism and homophobia. The angel let me see how I had wasted so much of my life by running away from this sacred mission. Then it gave me another message that I relayed to Doc. With its voice came my voice: 'You have sought oneness and harmony with God in the highest of places. You have taken the highest roads and pursued the highest of truths. But you must realize that God is not only to be found in the highest of ways. God is also to be found in the least of these.' Immediately I knew who the least of these were for this lifetime. They were the gays who were suffering as never before in history. And why? As a punishment from God? No. AIDS is not a disease just of the body; it is also a disease of spirit and mind. The disease is here only to force all of us to deal with the great disharmonies that we had created over the centuries. It is here to help us focus on our own evils that we had created in separating the masculine and the feminine in ego-based ways. Such things were never meant to be separated as if by war. They were meant only to be in balance, in harmonious equilibrium with one another. We are a patriarchal society that has disenfranchised women along with the feminine within men. We have ravaged the Earth out of a sense of ownership and egotistical power. We came here to be stewards of this Garden Planet, not rulers. I realized the importance of my mission as Doc continued counting. The more conscious I became the more anger rose up in me. What gave Doc the right to end the session? What if the angel had more to say to me? As I looked at Doc, I was about to chastise him for his actions when I noticed a light to the left of me in the corner of his office. As I turned my head, there it was: the angel. Standing there as big as life in all its splendor, its head just barely touching the ceiling. Was I ever relieved. I could tell Doc was puzzled by what I was staring at. That is when the next message came forth. The angel said to me, 'You have abandoned your purpose. You were born into a gay body for a divine reason. Yet you have fled that reason.' It was like being struck by lightning." Gary checked Nick's body language out to see how he had reacted to the revelation.

"And you were married at this time?"

"Uh huh. I was in my fourteenth year of marriage. The consequences of what the angel had said crashed in on me like a falling building. My first reaction was that of horror, not because I had been 'outed,' but because of the immediate realization of how many years of my life had been wasted. An unspeakable shame flooded me. I don't know if there is anything worse for a man than to realize he has wasted his life. The sorrow shook me, and I began to weep uncontrollably. Tears that had not been shed for the previous twenty years welled up and would not be stopped. Poor Doc. He had no idea what was going on. All he saw was this grown man bawling his head off.

"Then the angel did something very strange. It lifted its left arm to its side, the one made of the mother of pearl, and then swept it across its body. As it did this, an opening occurred, like a round doorway. And in the doorway was the God-Light. I hadn't seen that Light since I had drowned and died when I was eleven years old. The Light once again flooded me with love and let me know that I had been forgiven. The incurable disease was an effort to get me to wake up to my purpose once again. I had suffered enough. There was no need to suffer anymore. There was no need for shame, just self-forgiveness. I looked into the God-Light, feeling unmeasured gratefulness, but what I also saw was that even though the God-Light had forgiven me, I could not forgive myself. No matter how hard I tried, I could not forgive myself. And the God-Light faded. The third message came into my heart, like the previous times. I knew that I was to tell this story to five people, my closest friend and associates. And if they heard what I had to say and believed it, then they would be involved in the putting together of a company that would begin to change the days of suffering for humanity.

"It was then that Doc finally said something. His voice was quite shaky as he told me, 'Gary, you've taken a lot on. You don't have to take everything on at once. You can come back and we can discuss what has happened further. I'm here for you.' I turned to Doc and said, 'I know what I have to do.' And I did. As soon as the last word fell from my lips, the angel disappeared in a flash. Gone. Poof. Doc tried once again, 'You have my phone number. Call me anytime. You don't have do this all yourself.' And I told him, 'I know what I have to do. Let me pay my bill now. I won't be returning.' I paid my bill and left. Never to return."

"That's quite a story," Nick volunteered.

"I will understand if you feel the need to terminate our business relationship. My being gay could cause you problems."

"Doesn't change a thing as far as I'm concerned. I kind of thought you were gay anyway." The two stared at one another for a while appraising the consequences of the story that had just been told. "So, was one of the people you had to tell the story to your wife?"

"Yes. Having to tell her was horrific, but I did it. I let her know I'd give her a divorce if she wanted. But she wouldn't hear of it. She felt that nothing had changed. I was still the man she loved. As remarkable as that was for me to hear, I had to tell her that I could no longer hide who I was. I now owed it to myself to live the life I came here to live. What would happen if I met a man and fell in love with him? She quietly answered that we'd cross that bridge when we came to it.

"The other four people weren't so understanding. Only one of the four stayed friends with me. The rest were polite, but I didn't hear from them after that. So the company that was to be formed by their combined talents never came together. That's why I think your dreams of the Great Tomorrow are the second chance at creating a new kind of world that will allow the days of suffering to end."

"And the incurable disease?"

"A few days after leaving Doc's, I went to bed with the rash starting to cover my chest once again. This is when the itching is at its worst. By morning I knew I'd be covered in blisters. After putting on a new undershirt to prepare for the eventuality, I went to sleep.

When I woke up in the morning, the disease was completely gone. No sign of it. And it hasn't returned since."

"So what do you think the angel meant by your not being allowed to see your further purpose because of the possibility of misusing it?" Nick had shelved this question away ever since hearing that part of the story. He was determined not to forget it.

Gary paused a while before answering. "I believe it has to do with the information we are bringing to the world now. I believe we are to prepare the world for the beginning of the coming together of Heaven and Earth. For us to be able to be credible with others in this regard, we must be true to who we are, true to our hearts, and truthful in all we say. In this we cannot be afraid."

6

A Band of Seekers

hen Larry Marcy walks into a room, it brightens — no
matter how deep the darkness. How often has any of us
asked why terrible things happen to good people? If you were to ask
Larry about the terrible things that befell him, he would only look at
you with a quizzical grin and ask back, "What terrible things? I am
so blessed." Most would have thought otherwise.

In our hi-tech age of instant wonder and scientific marvel, we
tend to look to individuals of great talent, leadership, or power, to
act on our behalf. We elect presidents who we think can speak to the
world, yet we find behind the political facade mere men with human
flaw. And we become disillusioned, even cynical. Perhaps the reason
for this is our lack of recognition of our own circles of goodness,
fortitude, and marvel. And perhaps it is through people like Larry
that we discover the simple wonder and joy of being ourselves.

It is too tempting to look toward the highly gifted healer or the
charismatic leader to show us our intended paths. Oftentimes, with
angels in tow, it is far better for us to stumble along, feeling for our
path in the shadows of our own doubts and fears. For then we own
our self-discovery, we trust our own way. Larry was about to find

out that he was not alone on his journey, that there were others who would reach out to him, assure him he was, indeed, a light among lightworkers.

Brian first met Larry at one of the symposiums that Nick had presented. His inspiration from the event spilled over in his enthusiasm to Brian. "Just tell me whatever I can do to help. I'm willing to fold papers or clean trash cans. Whatever." The offer opened Brian's heart to the way Larry saw so much genuine goodness in the ideals of the Great Tomorrow. Any modern company would envy Larry's people skills, yet he was willing to perform the least flattering task simply to help out. Larry's generous heart, his affability, his capacity to include all around him in conversation and enthusiasm captivated Brian.

"You've gotta meet this guy," Brian had told Gary later. Little did Gary know the Divine Plan that would bring them together.

Over the Internet, and later in person, Larry had become close friends with a woman known on the Net as Angel Scribe. Anyone and everyone who had anything to do with angels knew Mary Ellen's reputation for being the Queen of E-mail. Whenever she signed her name, it was with a :) (smiley face) afterwards. She was either the grown-up version of Peter Pan or the embodiment of Pollyanna. Like Larry, she tended to see the best in everyone. But unlike any Pollyanna figure, she possessed the moxie of an Amazon. In other words, Mary Ellen could sell doorknobs at a teepee. Hers was the gift of gab, but God had balanced that out with a heart of gold.

Mary Ellen touched the entire world from the confines of her Gig Harbor, Washington, living room. Her computer hummed and buzzed from morning to the wee hours of night. For she had the innate calling and constancy of enthusiasm to send angel stories to an entire world day after day. The mailing list she had generated from her connects, most corporations would die to have. Silver-haired grandmas in Sun City, Arizona, as well as teenagers in the Bronx read Mary Ellen's angel stories about wanting to create a better world for our generation. Famous authors, promoters, and lecturers secretly resided on Mary Ellen's mailing list. So did ministers and celebrities. But most importantly, ordinary people read her angel newsletters regularly. And one of those people was Larry Marcy.

One day, unannounced, Gary received an e-mail from "Angel Scribe." Little did he know that her ebullient letter would bring a light into his world that would shine into the most unexpected of places. Like Larry, this Angel Scribe had read *The Messengers* and was promoting it around the world through her angel newsletters. She wanted to thank the authors, and she wanted to help out. At first, Gary responded in his typical fashion, thanking her, letting her know that many had responded in the same way, and that the staff at the Great Tomorrow was in the process of organizing ways in which to channel people's offers of help. But Mary Ellen would not let it rest. The experience of having been awakened at 4:44 a.m. the day after reading the book filled her with an enthusiasm that would not be denied. She sent a stream of e-mails insisting that her contacts could help the authors in promoting the books in the Pacific Northwest. It didn't take long for Gary to realize she should be taken at her word. And so a warm friendship and mutual respect blossomed as Mary Ellen buttonholed book-signing engagements for him and Julia Ingram as co-authors of *The Messengers*.

Mary Ellen's contacts amazed Gary. Not only did she introduce him to radio talk-show personalities, but also to bookstore people who believed in more than selling books. One such bookstore, Crystal Voyage, nestled in a renovated warehouse in North Tacoma that had been turned into a funky kind of mall. Gary thought Tacoma a strange city, despite its being his birthplace. Originally, it had been known mostly for its air pollution, branded by the entire state of Washington with the tag line "the aroma of Tacoma." But now, it had transformed into an emerging jewel since voters had decided to close down the smelters. The beauty of the Tacoma Dome stood majestically where once the heart of the stink had pumped. And as a further symbol of this new blood, stood a warehouse-turned-mall, named The Freighthouse Square.

Inside the all-wood mall, a smallish bookstore hugged against the planked wall with steel frames towering about the open ceiling. Most of the stores were merely partitioned sections, zigzagging back and forth through the length of the long, narrow freighthouse. As Gary stood staring at the store display of his book in the front window, Mary Ellen swooshed in, handing him information about his future schedules, books to sign for other promotions, and telling him about the old lady she had run into who had caused her to be late. It was another patented Mary Ellen angel story. This time the anecdote involved a senior citizen who had been caught in the rain, having had trouble crossing a street, handling packages and maintaining her balance, trying to keep her bounty dry. Mary Ellen had stopped to give her a hand across the street, and ended up taking her home.

"You will never guess what she said to me," the Angel Scribe gasped, taking just barely enough time to get her breath. "She said that she had prayed for her angel to help her out, because she had so far to walk. She had asked her guardian angel to bring the bus by, and then I showed up. After I took her home, she insisted I have a cup of tea. And of course I couldn't say no." Mary Ellen's sentences seemed to have no periods at the end of them. "She told me about her prayer, and how I showed up. She said to me, 'My dear, you are my angel.' Now isn't that just wonderful?" And before a word of answer could be offered back, "Oh my, will you look at that. Isn't that a great display the store has created for your book?"

"Well, they're not selling like hotcakes. I already signed what they had."

And before Gary could duck for cover, Mary Ellen whispered, "Watch this." With a voice that certainly must have shaken the warehouse skylights, she pointed to the book and pronounced, "Wow, you know, I've heard that this book, *The Messengers,* is a great book and an incredible read. All my friends have suggested that I buy it. What do you think?" Every head within thirty feet turned, including Gary's. Only he was trying to hide his blushing. This was so Mary Ellen, he thought. She was simply shameless. On the one hand Gary completely admired her ability to have no fear or embarrassment; on the other hand, he wanted to be in the next state, and correspond with her from this day forward only via the safety of e-mail.

It didn't take long afterwards before new e-mail arrived from Mary Ellen. "I think it is time you meet Atira," she insisted. "I think she is the most gifted psychic in the state, maybe the West. She would be upset for me calling her a psychic. She says that she is a 'mystic.' Like your Sara in *The Messengers*, Atira has the capacity to speak with the angels. And her angels are starting to tell her things about you and Nick. Perhaps you would like to give her a call" — the phone number trailing after the message.

As best friends, Atira and Mary Ellen competed as to which person visited the other the most between Gig Harbor and Seattle. Atira was a noticeable woman, her blond hair contrasting with her hallmark turquoise, large-rimmed glasses. Her talents many, she often traveled as a wholesaler through the Middle East or designed works for Universal Studios. She simply loved to walk in beauty, whether that beauty hung on a wall or dwelt in a heart, it made no difference to her. Hers is a heart of wisdom and kindness equal to the gift with which she has been blessed: her capacity to see and talk with angels. She uses her gift the same way Mary Ellen uses her communication skills to talk to the world: both are bearers of light into people's gray days. Both give beyond their means to others, and both love the comfort and truth of the angelic realm. They are a natural pair. The great contrast between these two women lies in their personalities. Mary Ellen can voice her thoughts to passing strangers, if she felt it would enrich their lives, while timid Atira carefully chooses when and with whom to speak.

Gary kept putting off a phone call to Atira, with more than enough filling his days helping to establish the Great Tomorrow, which inundated Brian and Nick as well. The new publisher fussed about planning a book tour, and Brian was the primary contact. Both Gary and Brian spent an increasing amount of time on the phone discussing concepts, strategies, and stories with one another. It was as if they needed to check in with one another just to stay grounded. Working with Nick was like rafting down one of Oregon's wild rivers. You hang on for all you're worth wanting to scream, "Stop, stop, let me off," and at the same time laughing like a kid on a joy ride, astounded by all the excitement around you, yelling "Don't stop, don't stop."

And so it was that Nick, Brian and Gary would find themselves on adventures in meeting extraordinary people. But perhaps more important was their continual discovering the extraordinariness in ordinary people. For the Mary Ellens and the Larrys are to be found across the globe. We have only to acknowledge them, choose to notice them. In American society it is too easy to focus on the hurricanes of the awesome and miraculous when we are truly in need of summer breezes that call us to our resting places where we smell the flowers, look at our own reflections on quiet streams, and know that God is to be found in the stillness.

Having witnessed Sara's gift of being able to converse with the heavenly realm, Gary was a bit suspicious that Atira might be another wild ride down an uncharted river. Certainly it could be fun, with new other-world scenery to behold. But it could also be another mind-blowing experience for which he just wasn't ready. His shyness and her timidity kept them from meeting, or even calling one another. Expecting Mary Ellen to settle for this was like expecting a pregnant mother to be content with delaying birth after the ninth month.

At one of Nick's speaking engagements, Atira "accidentally" bumped into Brian and Gary. Mary Ellen feigned complete surprise at the coincidental rendezvous in her most angelic way. Wasn't it nice that everyone was here? she had said coyly. And with exaggerated aplomb, she found an excuse to leave her best friend with her favorite author and his favorite friend. To Mary Ellen, this needed to happen. Simple. So make it happen. For a woman in her forties, she had more push than Sherman tank, to the point of repeatedly embarrassing her teenage daughter.

"Hello Sweet Spirit," Atira opened, shaking Gary's hand. "I truly am glad to meet you. And you, as well, Brian. Did you guys see what happened toward the end of Nick's talk?"

"You mean the emotions and the energy in the air?" Brian offered.

"Oh, no," Atira said with the kind of voice that wants to say *You poor boy, you mean you missed it?* "It was one of the most incredible angelic scenes I've witnessed in a long time." All of a sudden she had Gary's attention. "Oh, I hope I wasn't the only one that saw all those angels. I've never seen so many in one place. There were these magnificent creatures of light behind almost everyone in the symposium when Nick was giving his blessing, his healing of the spirit."

"Nothing surprises me anymore," Brian smiled with the kind of smile one normally sees after church. "What did they look like."

"Oh my gawd, they were so tall. I've not seen these kinds of angels before. I'm telling you this was some kind of special event. Angels are coming out of the woodwork." A kind of giggle punctuated her sentence. *What a lovely, innocent creature,* Gary thought, *but I need to go fold my socks.* She then turned to him as if knowing what he was thinking of her. "And I think Mary Ellen wants me to tell you about how *your* angels have been waking me up at 4:44 in the morning," she said to Gary.

No wonder Mary Ellen was playing spiritual Yenta, thought Gary. It was beginning to make sense now. "Really?" he murmured, stealing a glance in Brian's direction. Brian's eyes twinkled, wondering if the Mad Dog in Gary was going to come out.

"Yes, they have several things they want me to tell you, but most of it needs to be in private. I hope that is OK."

Brian patted his friend on the back with a "Go for it, big fella. I think I need to rescue Nick from the crowd. He wasn't even supposed to be out here after the talk."

Atira proceeded in telling Gary about the fate of *The Messengers,* as well as events coming in his direction. But most teasing of all was a warning about his driving. His angels were telling him to slow down. *Gawd, even the angels are complaining about my driving,* he mused to himself. On the highway, Gary truly became Mad Dog. His reputation as a driver was notorious.

"You need to be careful in the next two weeks. For there will be a car that will crash into you from the right side if you aren't."

That got Gary's attention. He actually drove the speed limit for the following week. But one night, while in a state of distraction, he entreated his friend, Jesse, to watch out for cars as he was driving, relaying to his friend Atira's warning. And not twenty minutes later, Jesse screamed for him to hit the brakes, barely missing an oncoming car … speeding in from the right side. If Jesse hadn't kept an eye peeled, the Volvo — the Sherman tanks of the highway — would have certainly hit Gary's car squarely. Atira and Gary became close friends after that.

As their two lives weaved together with each passing message over the Internet, Gary began to realize Atira's true ability. His growing admiration of her didn't stem from the fact that she could talk to angels, it was how clear her messages were. Like anyone else interacting with the spiritual world, she was not 100 percent accurate in all she had to say. That is to be expected when dimensions are crossed over or free will is engaged. What is understood in the world of angels is not necessarily understandable in our world. As Scripture warns us, "My ways are not your ways." And so it is. What also must be recognized is what weather forecasters call "chaos theory." As a weather front passes from one coast to the next, the breeze from the wing of a butterfly on the West Coast has the capacity of changing the weather pattern by the time the front reaches the East Coast. Similar affects are engendered with human free will as events come and go. But in spite of the random affect of free will, Atira's capacity to help people remained remarkable. One of her e-mail messages that particularly tickled Gary talked about how his angels had woken her up again at 4:44 a.m. "Can't you learn to talk to your own angels?" she had asked rhetorically. "I need my beauty sleep." And then she would proceed to pass on more information that left him scratching his head. *How does she do that?* he would ask himself.

A surprise message arrived at Gary's computer one night. "Sweet Spirit," it started in the usual way, "Spirit tells me there is someone you are to meet. His name is Dan McMahan. He gave me permission to tell you about him." She went on to tell of events that were approaching in which several people that Gary would meet would all contribute to the bringing forth of healing knowledge. But it was Dan McMahan that he had to meet now, she insisted.

"And just who is Dan McMahan? How do I even meet this guy?" Gary queried, wondering why there were all these people he had to meet of late.

The e-mail zipped by on a daily basis. In fact, Gary was beginning to wonder whether he wrote more e-mail than he did stories. She replied, "He's a very specially gifted man who can lay hands on people and help them in their healing process. He's read your book and is completely supportive of the messages within. He also feels called to help in whatever way possible in bringing forth the spiritual healing centers you mentioned in the book."

It had to be more than coincidence that these healers were appearing like, well, angels. These were not people who thought that alternative therapy was to replace modern medicine. They simply realized that even modern medicine had limits. People need more than diagnostics and prescriptions at times. We are more than just our bodies. Our emotions, our spirit, and our thoughts govern much of what happens to us. Any bright heart surgeon or respected oncologist knows that a patient with a healthy attitude has a much better chance of survival than a patient with an unhealthy attitude. A few hospitals in the country were even allowing Reiki workers into the operating room to support patients undergoing critical surgery. And now, medical research has proven that patients who are being prayed for have better survival rates than those who don't. Even patients who didn't know they were being prayed for do better than those who were simply left to the limits of medicine as we know it today. Atira and Mary Ellen had even set up such a prayer team, which connected over the Internet.[1] Gary was also aware that Nick was working with others in planning a center for healing of the spirit. The entire notion of watching all this unfold filled Gary with hope, and at other times with puzzling questions.

And one question that would puzzle him the most came in the form of a phone call from Atira. It wasn't a matter of this being a friendship of convenience for Gary, it was truly a friendship based on mutual respect. And out of that respect, Atira called to ask something of Gary he didn't know he possessed.

"Sweet Spirit," her voice sounding troubled over the phone, "I have a wonderful friend who is in need of help. I call him SpiritLife; that's his online name. His real name is Larry Marcy. I got a phone call that Larry is in the hospital. I've found out that he has suffered a brain hemorrhage." While helping a friend move, Larry had felt something go pop in his head. Apparently he knew he had hurt himself. As he sat down to explain it to his friend, she couldn't understand a word he was saying. His words were coming out all gibberish.

She had exhorted him, "Larry, I can't understand what you're saying. I want you to get yourself to a hospital immediately."

"Sweet Spirit," Atira choked, "I've found out that it's serious. Please, will you pray for him? He's is the most dear, sweet, person.

---

[1] http://angelscribe.com/prayteam.html

I'd be devastated if he left us. Please, would you pray to your angels to help him? Do whatever you can do, even if you don't know you're doing it, to send healing energy his way."

"OK, Atira, I'll do what I can. Are you going to be all right?"

"Oh, yes, I'm fine, Sweet Spirit. I'm just concerned about SpiritLife. He is such a dear friend. I'm going down to Portland in the morning with Mary Ellen to be with him, to pray for him."

"Can you tell me where he is located?"

"He's in a Portland hospital on the eastside of town. That's all I know. I've got the hospital phone number if that will help."

It was no secret that Mary Ellen and Atira had put together what is called a prayer line for just such occasions. Gary surmised that everyone on Atira's prayer line was being called this night. After he hung up the phone, Gary turned off his computer, bowed his head and prayed for this man he had never met, but seemed a part of his life by all he had heard from others. He prayed for this stranger whom his friend loved so dearly. Because of all that was happening around them, Nick, and Brian, Gary had learned to expect miracles.

The next day Brian called Gary on the phone to talk about the marketing of the book. Gary decided to ask Brian if he had heard about Larry's condition. He had not.

"Gary, have you met this guy?"

"Actually, I haven't. I've heard a lot of good things about him."

"He is something else," Brian continued. "Nick and I both have met him a couple of times. He has a heart as big as Mount Hood. I've got to go check on ol' Lar at the hospital." After calling the hospital, Brian told everyone on staff at the Great Tomorrow that Larry was in trouble. Hold him in your prayers. And off Brian went to visit the man of a thousand hearts.

Brian tried to be cheery as he stood next to Larry's bed. "Lar, ol' buddy, how ya doing?"

Larry, looking gray as a fence post, offered the answer one would expect from one such as he. "Oh, hi, Brian. I am so blessed. The people here are so wonderful. Atira and Mary Ellen were here earlier. I'm so lucky to know people like you. Life is so good." Brian winced at the slur in his speech and the slowness of the words. There had obviously been some brain trauma. Brian sat himself down and took Larry's hand in his. The clamminess betrayed the truth of the tough night Larry must have gone through. Brian teased him a bit, knowing how Larry would turn the tease into positive counterplay. Brian loved to witness this magic in his friend. And as if on cue, Larry turned his focus to the old guy in the bed next to his, trying to emotionally take care of the old buzzard, cheer him up. The old guy responded right away, asking if Larry could adjust the TV set for him. Brian forced Larry back to his pillow, then helped adjust the angle of the TV. Leave it to Larry to think of others when he, himself, needed even more care.

As Brian returned to his chair, the doctor entered the room with charts in hand. "Larry," he said pausing, "I don't know what to tell you. I don't have any explanation for being able to visit with you this morning; there's no way you should be here, actually talking with me."

"You mean I might have missed dinner last night?"

Brian snorted a laugh that said *I can't believe this guy. He should be dead, and here he is cracking jokes with the physician.*

"You mighta missed more than dinner, Larry" the doctor said in an almost soft voice. His eyes reflected the amazement he held for his patient. "Not only should you not be here right now, but I have absolutely no explanation for the fact that you can talk. I want to do some more tests and have you come back so we can put together a therapy program for you, as well as make suggestions as to how we can prevent this from happening again."

Brian thought to himself, *The power of prayer rules again.* After listening to the list of instructions the doctor gave Larry, Brian listened and then offered to help Larry any way he could. Shortly after, Nick called on the phone checking in to see how Larry was doing. Everyone who knew Larry offered help. Was there anything they could do? Of course, Larry's only wish was to get out of the hospital. And since the doctor could give no compelling reason for him to stay, Larry walked out of the hospital that day. The doctor wasn't the only one shaking his head in wonder.

After returning to the office, Brian relayed the story back to Gary. "This is simply amazing. You've got to meet this guy." Brian echoed what was becoming a repeating message. Gary decided maybe it *was* time to meet this Larry character. There was some magical trait in

Brian that constantly connected him with remarkable people. Perhaps Brian's heart, also, was as big as Mount Hood. There was no one who met Brian who did not sense his love, his peace, and his genuine concern for all around him. There was no denying that Brian walked with the angels. And if he insisted that his friend should meet Larry, then it simply must happen.

Upon their return, Atira and Mary Ellen burbled with delight over Larry's miraculous survival. Thank-yous were sent out to all on Atira's prayer chain. Mary Ellen relayed the event around the world through her angel newsletter, telling what their prayers had accomplished. *What an age we are in*, she thought, *When else could you ask people from around the world to pray for a single human being at a moment's notice?*

A week later, at Atira's insistence, Gary had arranged to meet with Dan McMahan in the Portland area. A mutual friend, author Joe Irgovich, would be in town, and all sought out each other's company. Mary Ellen had sponsored Irgovich in the Seattle area promoting his author tour, helping out as she had for Julia Ingram and Gary. Upon hearing that Joe was flying up for a talk at the Living Enrichment Center near Portland, Mary Ellen called Atira and another friend, Corey, who also knew of, and wanted to meet, Joe Irgovich. Before they knew it, a crew of six people were headed toward Portland on the same day. Dan would rendezvous with the rest at the Center.

Gary then called Larry Marcy from Seattle to ask if Larry was well enough to receive visitors, since Gary soon would be heading to Portland. Upon hearing that several mutual friends also were traveling to Portland to meet with Joe Irgovich, Larry decided to impose, for he knew of Joe's story. Polite and complimentary as always, Larry chirped over the phone, "Gary, I am so happy to get a call from you. It would be wonderful to see you. I've heard so much about you. I've also heard so much about Joe from Mary Ellen; would it be possible for me go with you folks to the Living Enrichment Center for the book signing?"

Was this a good idea? "Gee, Larry, are you well enough to drive?"

"No, but my mother is here with me, and she needs to get back home. It would be easy to have her drop me off and rendezvous with you wonderful people, if someone could bring me home afterwards."

Let's see now, Gary thought, *you've just had a death-defying experience, just left the hospital. Your mother is there to help you take care of yourself, and you want to go galavanting all over tarnation?* Gary arranged to meet Larry at the Crown Plaza, next to the freeway, in Lake Oswego. So, not only would Larry receive visitors, he would also be counted among the visiting.

A bright sun warmed Atira, Mary Ellen, Corey, and Gary as they reposed on the lawn outside the hotel. They figured Larry would be able to spot Mary Ellen from the car upon his arrival. Her rich, flowing hair and her typical springlike colors made her a walking vista. The grayish-white streaks highlighting her mane, her conditioned body, and her flowing dresses, all contributed toward giving her the appearance of those she most admired — the angels. The grass smelled freshly mown, the shade of the trees soothing, as conversation drifted around Larry and all he'd been through. Corey had not met Larry, and listened attentively to all that had transpired over the last month.

"You know, Sweet Spirit, I'm a little concerned," Atira mentioned.

"Why? What's going on?" Gary knew his friend well enough by now to know the angels had said something to her. Atira's ability to hear angels rattled even the most skeptical.

"Well, Larry had an appointment this morning with the neurosurgeon. And I am hearing that he is going to have to have major brain surgery. He's been through so much already. My guides are telling me that he may elect not to have the surgery, that he may decide it is not worth the agony. He has had such a good life that he knows he can pass over without regret. I feel he has so much more he can do on this side."

There was a stillness in the group as a swallow darted silently overhead. Gary pulled at blades of grass and lifted them to his nose to smell their aroma. "Well, maybe we might have something to say about that." His eyes looked off into the distance, as if spying on the statue of the Angel Moroni standing atop the Mormon Temple across the highway. Atira stared at him, saying nothing. She reached over and patted him on the shoulder. She knew what he meant.

"Hey you guys," Mary Ellen interrupted, "Larry should have been here by now. Do you think someone should go looking for him? Maybe he's in the hotel lobby."

"You'd think he would have seen us here on the lawn," Corey offered, shading his eyes from the afternoon sun. Nothing was stirring that might hint at a visiting car. Corey didn't want to be late for his meeting with Joe Irgovich. Like Irgovich, Corey had been awakened one night by a bright light surrounding a human figure. It had called out his name. As he bolted upright in bed, the figure had faded from view. Ever since that night, he obsessed over what the appearance had meant. Perhaps Irgovich might offer some assistance since he had gone through the same kind of experience.

"Mary Ellen, why don't you go check," Atira suggested. "We can watch for him from here." And off the earth angel glided, her hair and dress fluttering behind her.

"There's something about Dan you should know," hinted Atira. Gary turned his head to her, thinking, *What now?* She was always surprising him. "Dan has a special gift, as you know," she continued. "He asked me to do a reading for him a while ago. And his angels told me that he had the hands of the Master. Do you know what that means?"

"I can guess," Gary answered. Corey's ears stuck out like a horse's, listening for the arrival of an oat bag. Apparently, this gathering of new friends held more than eyes could behold. Perhaps he wasn't the only one here on a quest for understanding the weird.

"His angels told me that he doesn't fully know or understand his gift, yet, but that he can call upon ..." She decided to just say it, "That he has the hands of the Master when he works on people; he can help them heal. He doesn't even have to be in the same room to do it, or even the same state. It will take him time to fully comprehend this."

"Have you told him?"

"Yes. He was embarrassed at my mentioning it to him."

"And you called him the night Larry almost died? Asking for his help?"

"Course," she said, meaning *Do you think I'm stupid?* "I called everyone I could think of. It was a group effort."

A few minutes later, Mary Ellen returned with Larry in tow. He held fast to her arm as he shuffled along beside her. Gary could tell that his steps were short and deliberate, caused most likely from the brain trauma. His appearance was that of part Eastern wise man, part Native American shaman. His hair, neatly tied into a long, dark-brown pony tail, framed eyes that could melt icebergs. He was as Gary had imagined: Larry walked in the presence of love. Introductions were made, and as Gary crushed the marigold shirt of his new friend with a hug, he could feel the tremors rippling across Larry's torso. Just sensing the twitching muscles filled Gary with empathy for what this marvelous man must be enduring. "Larry, it's so good to have you here."

A great smile beamed across Larry's gentle face. "I am the lucky one," he almost sang. Even in his struggle with speech, Larry seemed to make the words sound like carefully constructed poetry rather than halted speech patterns. It was as if this man was incapable of anything negative. "Life is so rich," he crooned, "What an honor to be with such wonderful people. I am so happy!"

Gary had to turn his head so as not to show the emotion flooding him. His heart ached for Larry's troubles. And his mind reeled at how this man could possibly stand there and convince the rest of them that he was, indeed, lucky — one week removed from a brain hemorrhage that had almost killed him, leaving his body and his mind traumatized, yet finding life to be so rich. If he had not seen the man in person, he would have thought him surely to be a cartoon. Unable to speak, from the rock in his throat, Gary glanced over to Corey, whose mouth was hanging open, apparently with delight at seeing such rare people. He was basking in the light of these amazing souls. Though he had shaded his eyes from the sun's brightness, this other kind of brightness he could not and did not want to shade. *What planet did these people come from?* he asked himself.

"How did your session with the doctor go?" Atira asked with a twinge.

"Oh, he's a really nice guy, but he wants to cut my head open. Basically, he wants to rearrange the blood vessels on both sides of my head. It could eliminate the source of the blood-vessel problems. Or not." His hesitation betrayed the seriousness of what could happen. "So, I do have options," he concluded, his eyes looking back into the concern of those around him.

Atira owned up, "I'm afraid I knew they were going to want to operate. You know we will be with you through all of this."

Emotions rose up in Larry's face. "Thanks. That means a lot to me. I need to get a second opinion on all this." There was no more to be said. Larry was here for some fun, so let the fun begin.

As the crew piled into cars to head down to Living Enrichment Center, conversation focused on meeting Joe as well as Dan. While Larry sat next to Corey, Corey's professional eye caught telltale signs of Larry holding significant pain. "Are you doing OK?" Corey asked in his caring way.

"Actually, I'm having some real painful back problems. I think it was from lying so awkwardly in the hospital bed."

"How about I work on you when we get to LEC? I'm a doctor of Chiropractic. I believe I can fix you up, if we can find a table or a good place for you to lie down."

"That would be great," Larry purled, a brightness glowing on his face. "I'm so lucky," he began again, after a pause of thoughts. "So lucky."

The Living Enrichment Center nestled itself in farmland south of Portland, standing like a concrete Haystack Rock among a sea of fields. Simply put, the complex of buildings was huge. No wonder the place had the reputation for having the largest Sunday gathering of worshipers in the Northwest. As agreed, the gang of well-wishers waited at the front entrance for Joe and Dan while Corey went inside to see if a spare room could be found for working on Larry. Dan's arrival erupted into a family reunion. The hugs and gleeful words carried the evidence of common goodness and joy these people had for one another and those around them.

Corey emerged from the building with news of finding an empty room. As the gaggle of friends waddled down one of the grand staircases into the Garden Room, Atira began softly weeping. "What's the matter, Atira?" Gary whispered his right arm trying to comfort her. The building carried a kind of architectural sacredness to it, teasing him with the feeling he was in church, when in reality this part of the main building looked more like the entrance of a large bank building fashioned of formed concrete. Their voices echoed from canyon walls, especially since all the conference attendees were presently in classes. The bookstore appeared less a store and more an island in the cavernous midsection of the main building. The only way to know there existed a bookstore and not a library alcove was to observe the sales people and the book-signing area.

"Sweet Spirit, if only you could see what I'm seeing. The light coming off all you people is magnificent. I've never seen anything this beautiful before. It's like fireworks on the Fourth of July ... only indoors." Gary gave her a gentle hug as they entered the Garden Room. They immediately understood where the name had derived. A wall of glass opened to a walk-around garden of trees, shrubs, Zen fountains and statuary. With its overstuffed sofas and brightly patterned chairs, the furniture in the room gave one the feeling of being at home. Corey had already started working on Larry. Atira's weeping moved into awe as she gazed around the room at the "fireworks." After she and Gary planted themselves next to Dan on a sofa, Dan leaned over to Atira and whispered, "My gawd, what great energy." Gary felt left out of the light show. All eyes focused on Larry who was now replacing Atira in the weeping department.

"Life is sooooo rich," his words straining to escape his throat. "I can't believe I'm with you people." Corey grabbed Larry's right hip and shoulder and with a snap that all could hear relieved Larry of his back pains. A gasp of half-groan and half-ecstacy rumbled from Larry's throat. "That feels soooo good," he stage whispered, causing more tears to jettison from Atira's eyes.

Mary Ellen leaned over to Atira and murmured, "Am I crazy? I smell sandalwood."

"No, dear, you're not crazy," Atira choked out, hands covering her face, "That's a sign that healing masters are present in spirit." After composing herself, she leaned over to Dan, "I think you and Corey should work together on Larry." Taking Atira's cue, Dan and Corey moved Larry to a more accessible position, while the roomful of people joined together in sending Larry all the love they could muster from their hearts. One didn't need to be able to see invisible fireworks to feel the rapport swirling in the air. All were deeply moved in their desire for this treasured creature to be well. Larry lost complete control of his emotions. His convulsive sobbing only added to the bonding effect of the moment. Corey and Dan started sweating. Profusely. One would have thought the two men were working in a steam room instead of the Garden Room. Heat could be felt in the air itself, affecting everyone. Mary Ellen's eyes goggled. Gary reddened, but this time not from blushing. The formation of people around the sobbing Larry remained statuesque as if courtyard candidates for the garden. No one breathed, no one said a word.

Five minutes passed when Dan took a deep breath. "There," was all he said, his signal that the hands of the Master had left him. Somehow, he knew, on this unexpected occasion, he had not been the only one to feel these "hands." It showed on the faces of everyone there. Larry continued softly sobbing for several more minutes, interrupting his weeping with intermittent variations on, "I am so blessed. Life is just wonderful." His hands wiped his eyes as emotional gratitude poured out. "Life is sooooo rich. Thank you. Thank you."

As quiet as a prayer stood Joe Irgovich witnessing all of this. He wouldn't have missed this scene for all the avocados in California. Not much was said for a while, until Mary Ellen broke the silence. "Hey, everyone, Joe's here." After Larry regained his composure, the room became a festive reception area instead of a hiding place for amateur healers. Joe became the recipient of hugs and chatter, well wishes and how-are-yous. The afternoon wore on as the Garden Room became less and less private. Classes were out. Joe would have to return to the room in which he was giving his lecture. It was time for good-byes.

As the visitors got ready to pile into their cars, Corey invited everyone to drop by his mother's house for Chinese dinner. Corey's mom was a speech therapist who had volunteered to work with Larry while he recovered from his mishap. No one really wanted to leave the others. Larry spoke for everyone, "I think it would be perfect for all of us to have dinner together."

Gary noticed immediately that the slur was gone from Larry's speech. He wanted to talk to him more to see if it was his imagination. "I'm sorry, gang, I've got to give a talk to the Oregon Writers Colony right after this. I won't be able to make it," Gary said. Should he say anything to the rest about his observation?

Larry asked, "Whose car should I go in?" and Dan volunteered. As Larry walked down to where Dan had parked, it was obvious to Gary that Larry's shuffle also was gone. He was walking normally.

Why wasn't anyone else noticing? He wanted to run over and give Larry a hug to see if he still had his tremors. But all he could do was stand there with goose bumps camping out across his body. Maybe it was just his imagination. *Let it go*, he thought. *Wishful thinking.* Before he could say anything more, doors slammed, and cars full of hungry passengers set out in wagon-train style, destined for the Chinese feast.

Introductions were made and dinner ordered. Corey's grandmother and mother were delighted to have a houseful. All had been overwhelmed with the events of the day. Mary Ellen kept looking Larry's way every time he spoke, noticing the growing ease in his speech. With each sentence his words sounded increasingly normal, the delivery of his speech flowing at a normal rate. Unable to contain herself any longer she blurted out, "Does anyone else notice the difference in Larry's speech?"

"Well, I thought it might be just my own high hopes," said Corey, "but I've noticed it, too, Mary Ellen."

Corey's mom joined in. "I can verify that it is obviously better," she said with the authority of a speech therapist, "much better than last time we talked. Larry, what has happened?" Had she not, one week earlier, determined he could work with her in speech therapy? What had happened, indeed?

"It is the love of these wonderful people," Larry confessed. "They have supported me since this all began. I am so blessed to know them, so blessed. What have I done to deserve you people?" The house fell silent as six sets of eyes searched other searching eyes. The entire group then started to talk all at once, how they had noticed the improvement and been too shy to mention it.

Dinner arrived, the table was spread, and everyone gathered round. Stabbing at the selections with chopsticks, the tableful of visitors could speak of nothing else but the wonderful meeting and seeing Joe Irgovich at LEC. Corey's mother and grandmother felt like they had adopted a new family. Where had Corey managed to find such a group of people? For the next few hours all talked on how Spirit had provided the miracle of their coming together, working with one another, how precise the Divine timing had been at every step of Larry's incredible journey.

Only Larry could put the moment in true perspective. "You know, it's amazing what can happen when people come together. Life is so rich. You just have to savor it."

All were smiles. Larry was right. Grandmother gazed over at Corey and, with a wink, let him know she approved of his marvelous friends. Everyone seemed to be savoring the meal as much as Larry wanted them to savor life. No one wanted to leave the magic of the moment, for the conversation was a witnessing of the rapport that had overtaken all of them that day. The unconditional love of the group, the feeling of oneness, the work of the angels that had brought them all to a common path none wanted to leave, all this had created a moment none would ever forget. In the months that would follow, Larry would find that his healing path would include brain surgery. But like these people who surrounded him with their different gifts but common purpose, he would serve as an example to all how we as humans can heal one another in many ways. There is no one way to bring the fullness of life to us. Like the many choirs of angels, we are a many-splendored people, endowed with great capacity to foster manifold blessings upon one another. Sometimes, we need people like Larry to remind us of that.

Over the ensuing weeks, Larry went two dangerous brain surgeries. Vigils at the hospital had been planned, as well as the prayer chain notified of the upcoming operations. In each case, he amazed both friends and doctors, especially during the second surgery. Not only had his doctor marveled over the lack of swelling and side affects, but all who knew Larry were astounded each time he had walked out of the hospital after only a few days of recovery.

The circle of Larry's friends could only wonder at the blessing in their midst. Larry's continued litanies of "how rich life is ... I am so blessed ... what a great world we live in ... I am soooo lucky" continued to affect everyone around him. Many would shake their heads with smiles on their faces. Was this guy for real? Didn't he watch the evening news? But the five people who had bonded with Larry at the Living Enrichment Center could never forget what he had shown them. To a person, each admitted that they truly believed in the coming of a greater tomorrow.

SHEKINAH MINISTRIES

*T*he pages of Nick's journal were like time capsules of events from the past catapulting hints of our coming future. He was meeting phenomenal people laying the groundwork for organizations, ideas, and movements that will eventually prepare us for coming days of need and wonder. Leaders blessed with talent were networking with others who see a bright light shining within the heart of our nation. But besides those who would eventually move among crowds, there were also those, as well, who work with the few, who influence the fabric of life one thread at a time. One such person was Melodie Blair, a dynamic, powerful woman with a gentle spirit, endowed with seemingly endless energy. Initially, Nick heard about her through letters from others. Eventually, he received a personal letter from Melodie inviting him to pay a visit. It was a visit he would inscribe in his angel journal, for hers was a story that left him with his head shaking in amazement.

A lean woman with a youngish face for her forty-something years, Melodie's beauty flowed from her soul and through her eyes. She could easily pose for a painting of *Madonna and Child*. With her two sons, one twenty-one, the other fourteen, she lived in a house that seconded as a children's crisis center. Every inch of the two stories had been put to use in helping others or teaching others how to help one another. On this occasion the two met over lunch. Melodie ate like a sparrow, her attention focused on Nick as he told her his story. Then it was her turn to captivate him with her own storytelling. Either of them would have seemed like contestants at a liars convention. But what they spoke was the truth.

From the time she was three years old, Melodie remembered being consumed by a purposefulness, a strong desire to help children, numbers of children. Even as a youngster she kept seeing herself surrounded with children. Her mother would listen as her tiny daughter would insist she knew exactly what she was going to do when she grew up. Throughout her childhood she remembered always having this inner conviction, a strength in the heart, which left her with the capacity never to sway from the path that would lead her to a future few could survive. She needed approval from no one, so stalwart was her sense of purpose. From the time she was little, she remembered seeing her friends, the angelic beings, particularly around the age of eight. Like most precocious children, oftentimes she would share these events with her mother who feared for her child's sanity. Her mother would walk around he young daughter's room, night after night, touching along each of the walls to illustrate a point. "No, Melodie," she would insist, "there's nothing here!" Melodie would stare, wondering what Mother could be talking about, watching the angels stand next to her as well as her Mom.

As the years passed, the child became a young woman who finally questioned whether there really were invisible friends there. After all, she seemed to be the only one who could see them. To cope, she convinced herself that these beings were figments of some kind of claustrophobia, for she did have a tendency at times to bury herself in sheets and covers. Pressing a magic button that hid at the head of her bed, she would pretend to flip her mattress over, protecting her from an unbelieving world. But she never forgot her visions. Throughout her teens, Melodie worked with children however she could, finding particular comfort dedicating herself to the Big Sisters program, taking on a little sister, and helping families by caring for underprivileged children. Simply put, she adored children. And this adoration expanded as she entered her womanhood. "Are we not all God's children?" she would say.

"So you stopped seeing angels?" Nick interrupted.

"I chose to quit seeing them," she returned. "But not seeing didn't make them go away. Not seeing them made me increasingly aware of another kind of guidance, a guidance I would later call 'Spirit.' "

Though never taught a religion, Melodie had a strong spiritual life. Her family simply did not talk about religion. Such topics were not a part of her life, even though her father was an open-minded man who talked about there being more than the here-and-now. What she did hear and read about left her with an admiration, if not an attraction, for Jesus. He was the one example where she could innately feel heaven's ability to come to all people. What others told her about "God" simply did not register in her kind heart. *How could God be small?* she would ask herself. *How could God come to only one group of people?* It was a concept her child's heart could not accept.

"When I was older," she confessed, "I used to see light — brilliant, brilliant light. I would rub my eyes and look, and look again. What could I have ever done as a teenager that would cause this?" Little did she know how the angelic realm was readying her for events to come. At the age of fifteen, Melodie chose a future in personal development, taking a course from a professional school. Young women looking for careers in modeling or public life, typically enrolled. Rather than just completing the course of study, Melodie found herself literally rewriting the course. It was her first recognition that she was meant to be a teacher. And it didn't stop there. One day, in her early twenties, while teaching the course, she asked herself *Why are we waiting until we're teens and adults to learn abut how we carry ourselves in the world? Why not bring that to a child's level?* And she never looked back after that.

With her first son just over a six months old, an unfortunate marriage behind her, and five dollars to her name, Melodie began her own Montessori-like school. Her instincts were clear, and her cleverness legendary. Because she did not possess teaching credentials, she hired those who did, those who could train her so that she could acquire the knowledge she desired. She wanted her firstborn to live in a world that listened to children, nurtured the spirit of children, letting their desires blossom into whatever field of interest called them. The school acquired a reputation for its programs, which employed song, dance, music training, storytelling and whatever else was needed to empower the hungry mind of a child. Seven years passed, and to add to all she was creating was the arrival of another son. As with her first child she wanted to foster an environment that would bring fullness to this little life. Children were her life.

To further her own yearnings, Melodie started taking individual classes in herbology. She felt called to it. It was another tool that could be used in helping her own children. Deep within herself were planted hidden seeds that began to sprout as she became adept with her knowledge of herbs and their healing power. It all seemed too natural to her. Parents began to notice that their own children were unusually healthy, compared to their neighbor's children attending public schools. Melodie's growing knowledge of natural healing methods had become a part of her everyday life, and the children benefited. "It was a big draw to my school," she confessed, "along with everything else." Parents outside of the school began seeking her advice in how to treat their own children. Her reputation spread. She even began assisting doctors in family practice who had heard about her knowledge, her capacity to help children.

Her success with herbs matched her success with her school. It was said to be the largest home facility in the state. Nothing comparable existed at this time. She expanded her program into new areas with another facility, this time for infants and toddlers. With the emphasis on quality, rather than quantity, she began an out-of-home mini-center at a time when there were not yet laws or regulations to handle such a concept. It was at this time when she began experiencing what she called "dreams." To the rest of us they would be called visions. In one particular reoccurring "dream," she saw how her efforts would expand into a center dedicated to helping people grow, helping people to become whole. At this time, she had no concept that her dreams had anything to do with Spirit. It was later that she would fully understand that the center, itself, was to be a ministry of ministries, based on spiritual awareness. It was later that she would discover at the deepest level how people truly heal.

All seemed wonderful. Melodie's dreams were being lived out, her life with children fulfilling. "What happened then was like an initiation, a time of preparation before my awakening. To get to this point, my work was my life, I really dealt little with any kind of social concerns. I was in my school from the hours of 6 a.m. to 6 p.m.; then I taught personal development classes from 6 p.m. until 10 p.m. My role changed entirely in the evening hours, going from blue jeans and sweatshirts to impeccable professional dress. I taught professional modeling and personal development in self-esteem courses." Melodie's days were consumed with a constant outpouring of her mothering skills. Little did she know of the kind of strength and conviction that such dedication would bring. For with times of glory, challenge is usually close behind. When we find ourselves at the top of the ladder in life, all we have to do is look around, where, not far away, is inevitably a new ladder. And what we find ourselves staring at is an awaiting bottom rung.

Melodie's mother grew ill. She was found to have an inoperable, malignant brain tumor. Neither Melodie nor her mother knew of the trials the forthcoming months would bring. But one thing was clear to Melodie. She always believed parents raise you when you are little and in need. And when they grow older and need our help, then we are to care for them. Believing this, she took her mother into her own home, committed to caring for her. She knew her mother was getting ready to die. An independent, brilliant woman, the effects of the deteriorating disease now brought great frustration, confusion and anger. And as demands grew for more time and more attention within the home, pressures resulted from other sources. Clients began removing their children, thinking it would give Melodie more time. Others felt they did not want their children so close to death. Eventually, she had to let go of one of her schools, selling the home that had housed it. Though many would have found professionals to take over in such a situation, Melodie stayed to the end, lovingly holding her mother in her arms as she took her last breath.

But her mother was not all that died in her life. She found herself faced with a family situation resurrected from a Gothic novel. It wasn't so much the family drama that shook her foundations, but the adverse affect it had on her father. This man she had known all her life now claimed he was not, and never had been, her father. And with the claim came legal repercussions with the family trust that would cause Melodie to have to fight for her school and her home. Eventually, she could not, would not, go against her own father, disowned by him or not.

As Nick listened to her story, he could not escape the feeling of this woman's self-determination, her outright power of will. She did not just talk about her ideals, she lived them. Hers was a story he would have to remember, noting this meeting with her in his angel journal. This very thought seemed to take the conversation to the topic of angels. He watched her eyes fill with emotion as she unfolded a part of herself few were allowed to see.

As if heaven had other plans for Melodie, events took a bizarre turn. Doing a favor for a friend who needed help manning a display booth at a conference, Melodie found herself among people the likes of which she had never met. Human-growth workshops were going on in areas surrounding the booths where reps displayed products — in Melodie's case, herbal remedies. Strangers walked up to her asking if she did readings. She wasn't sure to what they were referring. Her exposure to the metaphysical community was nil. Seeking a place to rest while it was her friend's turn to take over at the booth, she found refuge in a lecture area partitioned off by curtains.

The conference half perplexed and half delighted Melodie with its strangeness as well as with its excitement. She had never been to a conference like this before. It was unlike any of the speaking engagements in which she had participated. A stranger, a lady from the conference, soon joined her in her hiding place, introducing herself. Both needed rest from standing at their respective booths. The two became rapt in conversation. Melodie began to share the story of what was happening in her life. As the two women delved deeper and deeper into their shared stories, the electricity from the conversation grew. They both became aware of an overpowering presence. It was the same presence that Melodie had felt before. It intensified to the point that Melodie felt she was being watched. And as she turned her head, magnificent creatures of light appeared before her. They announced themselves and began conversing with her, telling her of her purpose and events in her life that were yet to come. They told her that they were there to take her through an initiation. Specific instructions were relayed as to what she was to do. The presence within and around her grew so strong, "It was as if I were here and somewhere far away simultaneously. The information was long and so involved I could not remember or retain it all." For a woman whose life had been absorbed by the confines of classrooms and playgrounds, this seemed too much. She looked over to her newfound friend, who was overcome by what she had been witnessing. Tears streamed down her face.

Melodie said back to the angels, "This is way over my head. I do not understand."

One of the angels responded in a loving voice, "But you will," and both disappeared. The two women just stared at one another.

"Did you see all of that?" Melodie asked her companion, hoping her face was reflecting an affirmation.

"I not only saw it, I heard it. Who are you?" was the unexpected response. "You are so blessed."

What had happened was beyond logic, beyond describing, beyond their own believability. She knew she hadn't imagined the angels because the other lady had heard exactly what she had heard. The question still remained: What did it all mean?

The days that followed were days of wonder. The "presence," as she now referred to it, filled her with awe, reminding her of her favorite saying when she was a little girl: "I love being here, captivated by the color of the trees against the sky, the sound of waves crashing against the shore, or the song in a child's voice." How deeply she had been affected, even she didn't know.

Her peace was fractured one day, at school, by the scream of one of the little girls. Little Jackie had fallen and split her lip while playing in the classroom. The tyke was only a year-and-half old. Melodie rushed to the room to find the teacher, Judi, holding the toddler in her arms, trying to comfort her. Tears mixed with howling, her upper lip was already swollen twice its normal size and bleeding. Melodie's thoughts raced about trying to think what to do. A part of her wanted to take the child in her arms, another part argued, *No, I can't run in like this and take over as if I know I can do something nobody else can do.*

She stood frozen in self-controversy as the "presence" began flowing into her hands. While the electricity heightened with warmth, she realized she could not ignore what was going on within herself. Judi, knowing about the story of the angels, sensed something was happening to Melodie. As if by instinct she lifted Jackie up, carrying her to the doorway where Melodie was suspended. Almost automatically, Melodie reached out with her arms as if to say, *OK, I'll try*, not knowing at all what the results would be. Her heart opened with a hope, even a knowingness as she took Jackie into her arms. The child's face nuzzled into Melodie's right hand as she supported the toddler on her left shoulder. With the right hand covering the bleeding lip, the sobbing quieted with Jackie cuddling up against the nice feeling upon her face. Melodie and Judi conversed back and forth now that the crying had subsided. The tragedy had passed. Thirty seconds transpired before the baby turned her head around to gaze at her comforters. The bleeding had not only stopped, but the lip was completely healed. No split, no swelling, no bleeding. Nothing! "Did you see that?" asked Melodie, her voice almost lost. The women gawked at one another, stunned by what their eyes could not believe.

Judi's answer was a calm, "Yes, I saw that."

"You've got to be kidding," was Melodie's reply. Little was said of the incident. But its impact was profound for both women. Little Jackie had changed Melodie's life. The infant had taught Melodie not only how little ones don't carry patterns of disbelief, but also taught Melodie to expect the unexpected from that day forward. The school became a learning place of healing for Melodie in the days that followed.

As if to hammer the message home, another incident with one of the children occurred on the playground. One of the girls had been twirling around on one of the monkey bars, her knee hooked over the bar, pretending to be an acrobat. She had spun around the bar with increasing speed only to lose her grip and crash into the ground, knocking her unconscious. Melodie was immediately summoned as the teachers carried the girl into the building unconscious. It was apparent the child had suffered a concussion, her eyes rolled back in her head. Discussion ensued as to what to do: Put an ice pack on? Revive her, call an ambulance, or take her to an immediate care facility? And like before, Melodie became aware of the "presence" once again upon her. A hum moved into her hands and warmth filled her arms. The intensity of it surprised even Melodie. Instead of arguing with herself or denying what was happening, she simply said, "Let me hold her." Something within took command as she lifted the child up, laying her right hand on her head. The "presence" intensified like never before. Within a matter of seconds the little girl's eyes rolled back to normal, now staring up at her caretaker. With her own little hands, she grasped Melodie's hand and moved it to different areas of her head as if directing the healing energy wherever she needed it. The room was stone quiet. Nobody could speak.

Holding Melodie's hand to her injured head, the child began talking about the tingling she was feeling, and how she liked it. She wanted to stay in that feeling. And so they did, child and healer, locked in a knowingness. After a while, the child sat herself up, with nothing apparently wrong, skipped out of the building to return to the playground. She was fine. A while later she returned to Melodie's company. "I scratched my finger. Will you hold it, Melodie?" she asked, holding the small injury up for inspection. To this child, everything in her life was now open to healing, a testimony to suspending disbelief.

This time of initiation — the arrival of the angels, the growing role of healing in her life, the success of her school, and her own growing awareness — had altered Melodie's world beyond comprehension. "There was much I had to learn. There is a quote I like to use: 'Seek to understand before you seek to be understood.' It's the reason why we are all here together. If we were to come from a place of whole love, truly, and unconditionally — to seek to understand each other and the energy, that force which rises up in us, that determines the Presence we carry, that which we project — we would not have the discord, the disharmony we have in the world today. That is what healing is all about: Bones can move, split lips can mend before our eyes. Many things, which let us know that God is here working, can happen. But it's ultimately about us — every single one of us — learning to work in harmony with each other from a place of love."

The months passed as court dates and legal matters regularly interrupted Melodie's growing love of all that was holy. She had developed a deep and personal relationship with Jesus and with God. Those in the realms of the heavens had become her daily companions. Rather than spend any more time in court over who owned her house and her school, Melodie felt it was time to leave all that behind her. In contemplating what to do, where to go, and how to handle what life had dealt her, the voice of Spirit told her, *All things are handled in the kingdom of God.* She understood this to mean that she didn't want anything she had to fight for against her own kin. *You don't want to expend your life investing in such unfortunateness,* she realized. These are the roots of a society obsessed with possessions, willing even to go to war to protect them. Refusing any longer to battle in court, Melodie let go of everything: her beloved school, her house, her way of life. Now homeless, she felt God calling her to come to the mountains.

With the remaining cash she had left, a tent, camping gear, and sleeping bags were purchased. Moving into the Cascade Mountains, on a spot next to the Skykomish River, there she lived through the remainder of summer. Clothes were washed in the river's waters, meals cooked out of doors. Her oldest son stayed off-and-on with friends while she cared for her younger son in the wilds of Washington. Her closest friend left her, unable to tolerate her choice of poverty. He simply could not understand what she was doing, thinking she had gone mad. But these were times when Melodie grew closer to Spirit than ever before. Her choice was alignment with togetherness, rather than fighting in separateness. Her life served as a testimony to others she would come in touch with, from this moment on. For she feared nothing, least of all loss of materialism.

The voices of nature called to her about the harmony of all things. The wind in the trees whispered harmoniously with the chattering river about the oneness of life, while Melodie's heart yearned for a world of togetherness. She gave up everything she had because God had asked her to do it. And she responded wholly in faith. She considered it one of the most valuable experiences of her life. For she had overcome all adversity, chosen simplicity and poverty as her allies. The noises in the night served only to remind her to trust fully in God, to hear clearly the voice of Spirit. She would not fear.

As she discerned the next move in her life, Melodie knew she was not to plead for what she felt she needed. Instead, she was to direct her life, searching her own strength, and through such personal conviction, align her own purpose with God's presence. In other words, Melodie realized that if she was ever to tell her story and offer the lessons of life she had learned, if she was ever to teach again, it had to come from what she *knew*, and that had to come from her own experience. What she had to offer the world was her life, not her ideas.

"I was in a sink-or-swim situation," she told Nick. "I could not believe what was happening in my life. I began asking, 'Why is this happening to me?' I wasn't expecting an answer from God. But I found myself filled and surrounded with the most profound presence. The feeling of love was like nothing I had ever known before. I knew it was God."

This was the time of Melodie's awakening. The day was August 16, 1993, and she would never forget it. She had spent forty days and forty nights in the wilderness. Her days in the woods had brought her ever closer to Spirit and the purpose of her own heart. It was the voice of Spirit that spoke to her, telling her that her time in the wilderness was over, showing her how it was time to find a home for herself. She was told to simply place an ad in the newspaper stating her desires and what she had just gone through. How could it be so simple? Just put an ad in the paper? Her trust in Spirit lead her to do exactly that. A woman answered the ad and allowed Melodie and the boys to stay in a house. The condition was that Melodie would pay what she could, owing as debt what she could not pay at the time. It seemed that the goodness of others had answered Melodie's directions from Spirit.

Nick listened to all this, baffled by what he was hearing. This was a woman of singular dedication to spiritual awakening. He believed her words as she stated, "There is nothing but trust. There is nothing but faith. There is nothing but love. That is the true value of that time of awakening, preparation, and completion." At

Melodie's time of awakening, Spirit had told her that she would begin a ministry which she would call "Shekinah: A Ministry of Ministries." And that is exactly what she did. In the confines of a borrowed house, she drew together people of all talents. She would begin a concept that would be a model for others to follow, creating a oneness "on Earth as it is in Heaven." Classes were offered in varying fields, such as self-discovery for teens and adults, workshops on how to care for the elderly, presentations on transcendentalism. Spiritual groups were formed to educate people on the life of Christ, the life of Buddha, or any other religious discipline that interested folks. Others would come to the dwelling and stay with Melodie for different time periods for different kinds of healing. The house seconded as a retreat center. What had started out as shelter for her and her sons turned into a spiritual center for the many. It was like a multiplication of loaves and fishes, only this time it was a multiplication of talents and people who fed the minds and hearts of others.

Poverty was still Melodie's ally during this period. She asked nothing of anyone except what they could afford to give. And in several cases that was nothing.

As time progressed, she was once again asked by Spirit to move on. In this case she was directed to seek employment by finding a job in the newspaper, something she had never done before. She was to find work that would open her to her gift of healing. Her fingers searched down the want ads when Spirit told her, *This is the one*. It was an ad for a position as a nanny. "Spirit spoke to me. Sometimes I know things in advance, and sometimes I don't. This was one of those times where I wasn't told in advance. I just trusted." Even though she had never been a nanny, she knew this was where she would go next. Over 200 applicants sought to fill the job, Melodie being one of those asked to come in for an interview. While it took weeks for her interview to arrive, she left the borrowed house and the center she had created out of nothing but desire, and moved in with a friend, Mishe by name. Melodie had helped Mishe with caring for her mother earlier, and Mishe was now was returning that love.

Watching television was not one of Melodie's habits. In fact, she never watched it. So the interview did not prepare her for what was to happen. Her employer was a well known television personality in the Seattle area, who would later return to national prominence. They were looking for more than just a nanny for their child. "How do you feel about being in a home where someone is terminally ill?" asked the lady doing the interview. And Melodie smiled knowingly inside at Spirit.

"It gives me all the more reason to be here," she responded. The interview went far better than Melodie's lack of nanny experience might have indicated. Her work with children, her experience with Mishe's mother and her own mother made her a natural for the position, and it was offered. She would begin immediately.

After being on the job for four days, Melodie's work with the terminally-ill mother told her that it was more than just the mother's time to go, it was also the family's process of learning how to receive support, give support, caregiving, and the transition of life to death. Melodie and the dying woman hit it off right away. And on the fourth day she said pointblank to Melodie, "I know you were God-sent to me."

Looking into her warm eyes, Melodie responded, "You're right, I am." The relationship that followed became so strong that the daughter said to Melodie at one point, "You know, I think she really believes that you are her daughter as well."

During the days of horrible pain, Melodie asked the older woman, "Well, do you believe in ... you know ... healing through the hands — like touch?"

"You mean like pressure points or something?" she offered in return.

"Yeah, something like that," Melodie answered. She didn't want to go into any further in description, a little hesitant to do anything at all. But she knew she was here at Spirit's direction to help this woman. "Would you like to try that?"

"Sure" was the trusting response. And Melodie laid her hands upon the woman where the pain was the greatest. The pain went right away. The suffering woman asked her to try relieving pain in other areas, and the pain stopped there as well. Before Melodie finished, the silver-haired lady turned her head and stopped Melodie. "You can't disguise this," she said bluntly. "This is about

God." Upon acknowledging the truth, Melodie continued working on the ailing woman, relieving her of her chronic pain. After that, the two developed a marvelous relationship. They conversed about religion, ministry, the life process and all matters under the sun. It was a time of great growth for a woman on her deathbed. It was a relationship that Melodie would cherish forever. Like her own mother, the old woman died in her arms.

Employment as a nanny permitted Melodie to find her own house to live in. While she worked as a caregiver and nanny during the day, she continued doing healing with others during the evening at her own home. It was during these three years that she chose to become involved with some of the most needy and vulnerable in crisis situations, privately fostering children and families coming from abuse, drug addiction and alcohol dependency. Word of mouth spread, bringing more people to her door. She taught them responsible living and wholeness in life through spiritual conviction, creative problem-solving (placing the emphasis on the solution rather than the problem), and child/parent interactive guidance. Her work would become the foundation of Shekinah Ministries. Teenagers on drugs were worked with like no one had ever worked with them before. Not only was the addiction addressed through laying on of hands, but so was the source of the addiction, oftentimes a dysfunctional family. Because of her spreading reputation, crisis intervention became a part of the ministry to such a degree, that after her job as a nanny ended, she fully invested her efforts in helping children in varying ways. Her only limitations were the amount of space she had in her own home.

As she talked to Nick about her incredible life's story, it became apparent to Nick that Melodie represented the kind of work all of us may be called forth to do in the future: open our own hearts, our own homes to others. Melodie knew all that Nick represented in his own role before the world. And she wanted to leave him with a message to give to others. Her message was, "I call you forth as God calls you forth. And I say to you as God says to me: If you know the vision and you know the dream, and you do not live it, who will?" It was a statement that would remain with Nick as he continued to scribble in his journal, reading and rereading the stories of people he was meeting along his own journey. Melodie's challenge was more than words, her challenge was the calling forth of hope based on her own actions, her own humanness. "This is about coming out of ourselves," she said, "and joining together collectively, to create together, as an example to people all over the world."

As Nick closed this part of his journal, he reflected on all the different kinds of people he had met in his travels promoting *The Messengers*. Like Melodie, many others were in the process of starting centers or looking for others who might join them in manifesting their own ideals in some kind of communal support. As a businessman, Nick realized that the Atiras and Melodies, who were coming forward, had exceptional talent in communicating with the angels, with Spirit. The paths they had chosen were not paths that many could follow. It was too easy to dismiss such wonder as the unattainable, or even madness. The truth of the matter is that people like Melodie need help from others. She charged nothing for healings, relying on the donations of her clients and admirers. As a spiritual ideal, this made sense, but as a business reality it did not. People like Melodie often are in need of support, and don't get it to the full extent that their ideals demand. Even as all three, Nick included, embodied the ideal of once again bringing Heaven and Earth together, the fact of the matter is that the angelic realm seems far more supportive in this ideal than the earthly realm. But certainly, that is only an illusion. For the thousands of letters that had passed through Nick's office doors provided substantial evidence that there were those willing and able to support these ideals encompassed by emerging centers around the planet. There seemed to be a need for bringing these dynamic forces together: the willing and the able in league with the visionaries. There seemed to be a missing link. If the Great Tomorrow did nothing more than connect people of good will to those of integrity and gift who were capable of creating these centers, then surely that alone would be enough to change the world. Perhaps that's what Melodie was trying to impart in her own challenge: "If you do not live the vision and the dream, who will?"

DOWSING FOR ANGELS

*T*he Bitterroot Valley of Montana harbors the strangest assortment of human talent known to man. Along the shores of the Bitterroot River homes of the famous and obscure sit side-by-side, not unlike the diverse tribes of centuries past. For the valley was considered a sacred land, a healing land, where wars were not waged and intertribal trading flourished. To this day some of the best hunting and fishing in the world ranges between the banks of the river to the jagged peaks of the Bitterroot Mountains.

A day came when white men coveted the beauty of the valley and brought forbidden wars to the sacred places. Like the Cherokee of the southern Alleghenies, a Trail of Tears descended upon the Salish tribes of the Bitterroot as they were force-marched from their lands. According to local lore, an ancient curse hangs over the valley, incanted by an enraged shaman of that time. As the legend goes, the Salish would one day return and conquer the white man and his ways. Though you won't see it printed in the local newspaper, many of the folks who have moved into the Bitterroot Valley will tell you that they were led here for reasons they cannot voice. And some will come right out and swear they've been here before, the reincarnated souls of those taken from the healing lands of the Bitterroot many years ago.

One of those folks who will tell you he has returned is Michael Hoefler, a man of some legend himself. For Michael has made a name for himself as a gifted dowser and healer, and he will tell you that he once lived in the valley long ago as a medicine man of the Salish. Ask anyone who has witnessed Michael do his magic and a broad smile will stretch across their face. You see, Michael makes people laugh. All the time. His joke telling is as renowned as his dowsing. And when he helps people with their healing, one can't tell whether it's some kind of wizardry or the belly laughing that cures them. Of course, Michael doesn't care which it is, as long as people suffer less.

The first time Gary met Michael was at a speaking engagement in Hamilton, Montana. The local dowsers society had heard about Gary's work, his books, and his messages from the angels. Rumors from Missoula had reached the southern valley about an angelic gateway that opened the dimensions between the realm of humans and the realm of angels. Gary had learned the information about the angelic gateway while writing another book on angelic phenomena. Barnes and Noble had sponsored a book signing in Missoula at which a few of the valley's dowsers had attended. Now, if you haven't seen dowsers at work, you are in for an enchanting surprise. It's amazing the different ways these talented people divine information with their dowsing rods, or pendulums, or bobbers, or copper u-tubes, or coat hangers, or willow branches, or even their hands. One of the hand dowsers had attended the book signing where Gary had set up the gateway using seven different kinds of crystalline stones. During the talk and book reading, she had set her hand in motion near the gateway to measure the energy and the authenticity of the claims. It wasn't long before all the dowsers in the valley had heard about the phenomenon. Michael was one of the first to actually construct a gateway for himself so he could test what this creation was all about. Not long afterwards, an invitation was extended to Gary to speak before the dowsers society of the Bitterroot Valley on April 16, at Common Ground, a center for alternative events. And he accepted.

As Gary sat in the front row waiting for Michael to finish his introduction, a folded piece of paper emerged from Michael's vest pocket. "Well, you know I can't let an opportunity like this slip by without a joke." The audience immediately began tittering, knowing Michael had a joke for any and every occasion. "Gary, I hope you don't mind but I can't resist getting people into a good mood for your talk. As all of you here know, I've experimented with Gary's angelic gateway and have found the energy magnifies dowsing abilities tenfold. Amazing, simply amazing stuff. Gary will explain that later, if I ever yield the podium." Michael truly was a humble man who loved to be around people. And if people were around, that meant it was time for a joke: "There was nun waiting to catch an airplane to Chicago. She sat patiently with the boarding pass in her hand." Gary also sat patiently as the joke progressed. He noticed how Michael's eyes constantly scanned the crowd as if spying on any heart carrying sadness. Any hint of depression or sorrow and Michael's radar locked on. The scanning would cease, yielding to a concentrated attention aimed at the less-than-joyful heart. It was as if the dowser used comedy as his dowsing rod and his jovial antics as healing salve. Truth be told, Michael Hoefler had an uncanny resemblance to Howdy Doody, only without the strings.

"Well, being the punctual kind of person she was, the nun had arrived well ahead of the time needed for catching her plane. As she looked around the concourse she spotted a fortunetelling machine in the corner that also gave one's weight. 'I've never used one of those before,' she thought. 'Maybe I should try it.' So she moseyed over to the machine and stepped on the scales. She saw it took a quarter to get the fortune and her weight, so she fished into her habit and came up with a quarter, dropping it in the coin slot. A card popped out of the machine, and on it was printed, 'You are a nun, you weigh 122 pounds, and you have a flight to Chicago.'

"She thought this was amazing. 'How could this little machine know all this information about me?' So she put in another quarter, and another card popped out that said, 'You're a nun weighing 122 pounds, you have a flight to Chicago, and you're going to play a fiddle.' And she thought, 'No way, I never played a musical instrument in my whole life. This is wrong.' So she went back to her chair and sat down.

"Within a minute a man sat down next to her with a violin, and she asked him if she could play the violin. And he said, 'Sure.' So she played the violin like she had played it her whole life. It was just incredible. She went, 'Oh my God, that machine knows something about my life I didn't even know.' So she goes back over to the machine, stands on the scales and drops in another quarter. And another card pops out saying, 'You are a nun, you weigh 122 pounds, you have a flight to Chicago, and you're going to break wind.'

" 'No, I've never broken wind in public in my whole life. This is embarrassing.' So, as she's getting off the machine, she sort of stumbles and breaks wind. She is thoroughly embarrassed but says, 'I've got to check this out one more time.' She gets back on the machine, puts a quarter in, and gets a card that says, 'You're a nun, you weigh 122 pounds, and you've fiddled and farted around and you've missed your plane to Chicago.' "

After the laughter had died down, Michael endeared the audience further with his, "Gee, I hope that didn't offend anyone. If it did, I apologize." Introductions were made about the guest speaker, and as Gary approached the podium the applause resounded the welcoming environment Michael had created with his humor. What the attendees did not know was that Michael and Gary had privately agreed to do a co-presentation. For Gary had become quite amazed at Michael's capabilities. After talking about his work with Nick and the creation of The Messengers, Gary began presenting other sources of information about the angelic realm. Every eye in the crowd was locked onto him as he began to reveal prophetic messages regarding the coming together of heaven and earth. As part of that message, Gary began explaining the set of stones on the meeting room floor that he and Michael had placed before the talk. The geometry of the seven stones created nothing less than an angelic gateway in which man and angels could come together. It was at this time that Gary asked Michael to stand and speak about discoveries he had made about this new phenomenon.

As Michael got up from his seat, he began to pull objects from his satchel. He called the dowsing rods "L-rods" because of their shape, and explained to everyone how they worked in his hands. This was done for the benefit of visitors who were not yet acquainted with the world of dowsing. A bottle of water was placed on the floor with Michael backing up to make distance between him and the water. After asking the rods to show him the location of the water, he then ambled in the direction of the bottle and as he neared it, the L-rods swung to the center and crossed. He repeated the demonstration from the opposite side so all could see. Michael then described how he had taken this sacred geometry in which the stones were laid, and had begun to measure the energy emitting from the center of the geometry where the gateway resided. He explained to the audience that he had never seen this kind of energy coming from any other geometric object or grid. To illustrate this, Michael marched to the far corner of the room and asked the rods to show him how far out the energy from the gateway emanated. After taking only a few steps the rods crossed as before. A murmur began to rumble among the dowsers in the meeting. When it was explained that the geometric layout of the stones in the room was a smaller version of what the angels had given, Michael then disclosed that a full-size gateway had been constructed in the valley where he had tested the full strength of the gateway. The outer edges of reach of the full-size gateway extended as far out as 350 feet. Such power had convinced Michael to construct a gateway in his own apartment, enabling him to do his healing work and phone consultation work with far better results.

Gary peered around, watching certain participants pulling out their pendulums, most of them made of some sort of crystal dangling from the end of a chain. Their heads were nodding yes to everything Michael was telling them. The buzz grew as Michael continued. "What Gary and I would like to show you now is how this gateway can work with the angelic realm." Michael extended a hand toward Gary to continue.

"What we've found out is that this sacred geometry can actually be used in assisting us in better communicating with the angelic realm. Naturally, you can talk to your angels anywhere and anytime you wish, but using this gateway is like getting an especially clear phone line to facilitate the conversation. You will see that the geometry has seven places where you can stand. The place you stand depends on the creative energy or creative ray of light you were born under. Think of it as a different kind of astrology. Instead of being born under a star sign, imagine being born under a certain ray of light which determines what gift you carry, what gift you were born with. This gift carries a certain signature of energy. The seven rays are the seven colors of the rainbow. Let me illustrate."

Before the meeting, Gary had made arrangements to use Michael's wife, Jane, to show how the rays work. Using the dowsing tools, Michael had determined that Jane had been born under the green ray while he had been born under the blue ray. Those born under the green ray reflected the gift of those who mend that which is broken — or healers. Jane's gift was that of healing the environment, displaying this gift in an unusual way. Her artwork was well known around the valley. The pictures she created with her colored pencilwork almost always told a story about a particular animal, whether that was a totem animal or medicine animal. A story went with every picture, educating and encouraging people to understand the environment around them. The valley was sacred to Jane and she in turn was respectful of its beauty and riches. Her work had been dedicated to healing the environment and healing people's attitudes about nature.

As Gary asked Jane to stand in the position of the green ray in the south, he explained how Michael would stand in the west because he was born under the blue ray. When seven different people born under the seven different rays stood in the geometry, Gary explained, the angelic gateway would open. However, because it's not easy to find seven different people who can come together at the same time, the angels had given out information as to how the seven different stones (each a different color) mimicked the energy of the rays the people were born under. Gary then asked that the angels remove themselves from the gateway, causing a few in the audience to smile quizzically. Was this for real? We can ask angels to come and go at will? He then yielded the floor to Michael who explained, "I'm going to walk through this geometric construction to dowse, to test to see if any angels are present." With L-rods in hand, he made a beeline toward Gary right through the center of the angelic gateway. "As you can see, the dowsing rods don't move at all. No angels are present. Now Gary will call in Jane's helping angel, whose name is Gabriel. I believe this is the helping angel of greens, those born under the green ray?"

Gary nodded an affirmative. With certainty in his voice he announced, "I now ask that the angel Gabriel come forth to assist us." Now the interesting thing about dowsers is that they know energy, they sense energy, and they aren't afraid to let folks know they are using energy. "Whoa," could be heard from several dowsers next to the gateway. The audience was already being tipped off. "Now, Michael, if you would, please check for the presence of Gabriel in the gateway."

As Michael set the intention for his divining rods, he began his trek across the width of the gateway. About six feet before he reached the center, the rods crossed. He continued walking until he was about six feet beyond the middle and the rods went straight again. People in the back began to stand. This was not to be missed. Michael volunteered, "A pretty strong presence. I can see that some of you sitting nearby can feel it as well." Heads began to bob in the affirmative. Questions immediately followed about whether we can see these beings. Gary began to describe how we all have to start somewhere with a new phenomenon. When he had first worked with this geometry, he could see nothing, and he couldn't really feel much. But the more he worked with the energy, the easier it became to feel the presence of an angel and ultimately to start seeing them. He pointed out that dowsers usually have no trouble feeling or sensing energy, and that this was an exceptional group because of that. To make his point even stronger, Gary asked how many in the audience could see the presence as well as feel it. Michael and several others raised their hands. The rest of the audience sat captivated.

"So, like other alternate-reality events, the real question is how can we make use of this? Surely this phenomenon would make great party conversation or make one popular with the neighbors, but so what? Why have the angels given us this gift?" Gary paused a few moments to let the questions set in. "The angelic realm has stated purely and simply that they wish the days of suffering for humanity to come to an end. They wish that we prepare ourselves for the coming of a better world. And dare I say it? They tell us this world will be even better than the legendary Garden of Eden. So how can we use this gateway? First of all, we can ask questions or seek guidance by standing in the outside positions of the gateway. Let's illustrate." Gary asked Jane to voice a question that would have an obvious answer of no. This would help to form a dialog between Jane and Gabriel. The first trick was to totally focus on one's body, to become aware of one's feelings, senses, smells, sounds. Then ask the question. Look for any changes whatsoever to indicate whether a yes or a no was being given. He asked her to phrase the question in such a way as to not ask the angel how to live her life. Angels aren't here to live our lives for us. They are here to guide us and help us. We are not puppets; we have free will, which the angels honor more than anything.

Jane stated that she was getting a tingling in the back of her neck which told her that the angel was using that to give her a no. She next asked a question she knew would have a yes to it. This time her hands became warm. And to add to that, one of the ladies nearby commented she could smell gardenias. The participants began to understand that a "language" was being developed to establish a means of communication between Jane and Gabriel. Jane then began asking other questions, to the audience's delight. Pendulums were pulled from several pockets as many of the dowsers began checking the veracity of what was happening. There was little doubt on anyone's part that the angelic gateway was actually working. A broad grin spread across Michael's face as he began witnessing what he had hoped for: His dowsing colleagues would spread the news far and wide that the realm of angels has created a doorway to the realm of humans — a doorway that would facilitate the end of suffering for humanity.

"The second way to use this gateway is for receiving," Gary said. "To receive, one must simply stand in the middle. Jane, would you kindly take your shoes off and stand in the middle?" Doing as requested, Jane removed her Birkenstocks and tiptoed into the middle of the configuration of stones. "The center of the gateway allows us to receive whatever it is that we need: comfort, love, peace, healing, joy, calm, rest — whatever. We simply have to ask. It's a great place to meditate, allowing one to focus like never before. Jane if there is anything you'd like to receive, now is a good time." Jane closed her eyes and took several deep breaths. After a few minutes she simply said, "Wow." After a few more minutes, she opened her eyes to address the crowd. "You people have to try this out. This is great." Gary let everyone know that the talk would end soon and anyone who wished could then stand in the gateway. Gary requested that people remove their shoes before entering since they were entering sacred space.

Questions were taken as Jane returned to her chair next to Michael. The meeting had to be lengthened so all the answers could be addressed. No one left at the prescribed time. All attending wanted to know as much as possible about this new phenomenon. Gary announced that he and Michael would be attending the Spokane Mind, Body, Spirit Expo over in Washington State, and that a full demonstration of the powers of the gateway would be demonstrated there. The two had already agreed to present the information with a colleague from Spokane named Harvey Caine, a respected healer in that area.

As the meeting ended, folks flooded the gateway wanting to check out the energy, or what Gary had carefully described as "grace." Michael sidled up next to his co-presenter and whispered, "Pretty good, huh? We may be here all night if these people keep standing in the gateway." The truth was that those who had entered the gateway first simply did not want leave. A line had formed with those waiting to have their turn in the middle of the geometry of stones on the floor. All wanted to believe that the days of wonder, indeed, were upon us. The dowsing community of the Bitterroot Valley would never be the same.

Gary got to know Michael better as the date of the Spokane Expo approached. The more time he spent with the waterwitcher, the more surprised he became at how this quiet man had become aware of his gifts. Michael's life had been no more typical than the profession he now chose as a diviner and healer. As a sophomore in high school he first became aware that he knew things that his classmates did not. "We had a class in the library at school, and I was watching the teacher moving the desk, which had a movie projector on it. With a vividness that surprised me, I 'saw' in my mind the projector falling and crashing to the floor. Immediately, I started to get up to prevent the accident but then stopped myself, feeling awkward. It seemed so ridiculous to see with my eyes, you know, the projector sitting there. What was I thinking? As I recovered from my embarrassment, it happened. The projector tilted to one side and fell in a crash to the floor. After that I started looking at myself differently, and I began to examine how to use these warnings in a way that would not embarrass myself. In hindsight, if I had gotten up and simply said that I just wanted to make sure the projector was OK by grabbing ahold of it, everything would have been fine."

Baseball is one of Michael's passions, and after the projector scenario, he began to realize that he could see plays before they happened. And like the falling of the projector, it took him a while to begin believing he could act on these premonitions.

As was his way, Michael kept these awarenesses to himself throughout his college years, not wanting to attract attention or have people think he was different than they were. But in 1994, while desperately looking for work, he signed on with the Psychic Readers Network. It was also around this time when he started attending dowsing conferences. And to his amazement he discovered his abilities were greater than even he realized. His days with the Psychic Readers Network were enlightening in teaching him more about his abilities, but they also trained him to deal with the human condition in all its foibles and eccentricities. One of his favorite stories to tell involved an eighteen-year-old boy from Texas who called up wanting to know when he was going to lose his virginity. Michael laughs when telling of the conversation with the lad who was adamant about being deflowered. As their conversation continued over the phone, Michael began to see a scene in the back seat of a car that would occur in the month of June. So Michael relayed to the teen that he would have his first experience in three months. Hearing the cheers of the lad whooping over the phone made a lasting impression. The pressures of our society do strange things to us, and Michael had began to witness how we mess ourselves up in several ways, even to the point where people bring disease upon themselves. The Texas teenager never called back, which told Michael that the youngster had found his Holy Grail in the back seat of a car, as foretold. But what had the boy learned about love?

Another typical human trait Michael repeatedly scratched his head over was the client who would pay good money for advice and then not listen to it. Another Psychic Readers Network caller had asked which car she should buy. There was a particular car the lady had her eye on out of the several she had examined. She had driven a red car which she favored but wasn't sure if it was the right car for her, whether it was a lemon or not. Michael had dowsed for specific information and relayed to the woman that the car was indeed a lemon, that it would not be reliable. In his mind he began to see that there was another car at the same dealer's lot that was for her. He told her, "Go back to the dealer and have him show you three different cars. There is a GM car on the lot that would be good for you, a blue GM car. If I were you, I'd buy this one. But there is also a Ford and a Chrysler that you should look at in case you don't like the style of the GM." The lady thanked him profusely and went right out and bought the red car. The next day she called back asking specifically for Michael. After purchasing the red car she discovered problems right away with the thermostat. Upon taking the car to a garage even more problems showed up. What should she do? Michael wanted to yell at her that she should have listened. There wasn't much else for her to do except learn a lesson, take the car back to the dealership and ask for a car that worked.

Questions about medical conditions started to surface as Michael's reputation began to spread. His first efforts with dowsing came about by building what dowsers call a bobber. After attending a dowsing convention, Michael constructed his own bobber by stretching out a clothes hanger, keeping a curve on the end. He then drilled a hole in a little peg and stuck it on the end, fashioning his first high-tech dowsing instrument. It wasn't as if he were a neophyte to the world of dowsing. While growing up in Colorado, Michael had heard how his uncle had a reputation as a dowser. His mom had told the kids, "If you want to have a good well, you need to have it witched." The bobber became Michael's entrance into the world of dowsing. Watching it jump around while searching for water or looking for lost objects fascinated him. The instrument seemed to have a life of its own. As part of his expanding world, Michael began to experiment with healing energy. At the dowsers conferences they constantly stated that all of life is energy. And if it's energy, then it can be dowsed, altered, or healed with intent. Michael had met friends who did healing work, showing him how he could use his talent, as well as his bobber, to help others with their healing. His first client was a psychic friend who encouraged Michael to work on his injured back. Under the friend's tutelage, Michael discovered the bobber could transmit as well as receive. The friend's back healed with Michael's good intentions and strong ability to funnel healing energy. Little did he know that he would start down a path that would lead him to a world he never dreamed of. After lending the bobber to a lady friend who wanted to do some work on her property, the instrument was never returned. And just as well, for it forced Michael to begin working with pendulums, which were easier and faster to use. Jane created aids by which the pendulum could be used for discovering all kinds of information: dates, times, dietary needs, chemical imbalances, health problems, and even what food to eat at a restaurant. So familiar had Michael become with the pendulum work that he could be seen at a restaurant with friends, swinging the pendulum over the menu and ordering whatever it was his body most needed. Waitresses loved him. Took away some of their humdrum. One thing about Michael: Around him, life is never boring.

Gary stood in shock at the throng of people jamming the Spokane Expo. Over 15,000 people had shown up. And he had been billed as one of the main attractions. Twice the Expo staff had to move him to larger rooms to accommodate the crowds. Both he and Michael had to abandon their detailed planning to adjust to time changes and space constraints. Their main workshop had moved to one of the keynote speaker halls. Because of the unexpected move, they had to rush to construct the angelic gateway near the front so the audience could see what would happen. Harvey Caine had lent his own reputation to the three-man effort to show the people of

Spokane that a world without limits was more than a matter of dreams. Both Harvey and Gary took turns amazing the crowd with demonstrations, Harvey showing the immense role that love plays in bringing healing to our lives, Gary showing the crowd how the angels had taught techniques where water could be changed by blessing it with grace (divine love). He had asked for four volunteers to come up before the crowd. Each volunteer was instructed to randomly select from a case two bottles of sealed water, purchased at a local grocery store. One of the bottles was to be placed under the person's seat while the remaining bottle would be brought forward to be blessed. After blessing the four bottles of water, the volunteers were encouraged to then taste the blessed water, followed by a sipping of the unblessed water waiting under their seats. The stunned look on their collective faces told the audience everything. When comments were solicited, each volunteer expressed amazement that water could be made to taste so fresh, so alive, so sweet. The unblessed water, according to some comments, tasted like crap in comparison, with the taste of chlorine and plastic mixed in. Gary then asked for another volunteer to come forward who would be taught how to change the water in front of the audience, so that all would know that each of us is able to change not only water but also our bodies — even our lives — with these techniques. Are not our bodies made up of 75 percent water? If we can change the water in a bottle, then think what could happen if we changed the water within ourselves, the life forces within our bodies.

Now it was Michael's turn. After asking for a volunteer who had a medical problem to come forward, he instructed the lady to take her shoes off and step into the middle of the angelic gateway. Information had been shared with the workshop attendees as to how to construct their own gateway, how to use it, and how to place the seven different stones. Like before, the audience saw how Michael could dowse for angels, could help a person begin their first steps in learning how to talk with angels. But unlike the presentation in Hamilton, he would now show the participants how the gateway could be used in assisting people with healing.

The gray-haired woman standing in the middle of the gateway looked around wondering what she had gotten herself into. Her bright orange sweater acted like a neon sign as every eye in the conference room focused on what was going to happen. People in the back stood on chairs so as not to miss a single detail of this healthy looking, lithe older woman standing before them. Michael tried to put everyone at ease with a joke. Noting that the lady still exhibited a bit of nervousness, he followed up with another joke which got her to laugh. Then he began. He explained to everyone, "You will see that I use a pendulum as one of my tools to discover what is out of place with a person. As it swings in this direction I know that everything is in balance. If it swings the other direction, then I know work needs to be done." The rocking pendulum hung above the woman's head, indicating all was well. As Michael lowered the pendulum down the body the rhythm of the crystal on the chain did not change until it reach the groin area. "Well, uh oh," Michael politely stammered. "I guess we have some issues around, uh, relationship." The woman burst out laughing.

"Oh, come on, you can say it. I'm having more than a problem with my relationship; there seems to be an issue around sex. I like it. And I ain't gettin' enough of it." The crowd chuckled at her candor. A broad grin swept across Michael's face, which now turned a nice shade of crimson. He always tried to be respectful of people's privacy, especially in a public environment. But this lady didn't seem to mind telling her story in front of God and everyone. As the pendulum swept back and forth from the lady's left hip to her right hip, it once again changed direction.

"Yes," Michael confirmed, "the energy block does seem to be coming from a male figure. Let me see ..." Pulling out a laminated card from his shirt pocket, Michael began swinging the pendulum over the card. "Well, it looks like you and this man have past-life issues that are a part of this problem. And it looks like you are ready to let go of these issues even though he may not."

"Wow, you got that right," the lady in orange volunteered. "Do you think you could use that thing on him?" The audience rippled with laughter. They were caught up in the event, sympathizing with what this lady was facing and how she might deal with it. Michael always had a way of winning people over. The hall full of people was one with the woman in the middle of the gateway. As all waited to see what would unfold next, Michael asked the woman, "If you like we can ask the angels to help us here in ridding you of any past-life energy that is blocking you, and to remove any emotional baggage that may be affecting you."

"Oh, yeah, Darling, just do it!" she sang out. Again the audience tittered with laughter. Michael began focusing on the woman's abdomen and hips as if he were looking inside of her.

"OK, let's let this happen. I ask your angels and guides to assist you in removing these problems." A silence came over the room as the woman stood motionless while Michael focused on the swinging of his pendulum over the card in his hand. "I'm seeing that it's starting to happen. Your helpers are starting to move this old, stuck energy out."

"Oh my God!" the woman said in a loud voice. "I'm getting so dizzy. I don't get dizzy. What's going on?"

"You're OK," Michael encouraged. "It's quite common for people to get disoriented as this stuff moves out. If it gets too much for you to handle, let me know, and we'll back off for a bit."

"No, no, don't stop. I want this to be over with." Even Harvey and Gary were now standing to watch what was unfolding." My goodness, dear oh me," the lady stated in a heavy whisper. "I'm getting so hot. I don't do hot. I never get hot, Deary. I'm always having to get blankets to keep myself warm. That's why I'm wearing this heavy sweater, 'cuz I'm always cold. But now I'm starting to sweat. Look at me." Like a conductor before a symphony orchestra, the lady began pulling the sleeves back from the sweater, waving her arms for Michael and everyone else to see. "Honey, I don't sweat. Never. And I'm starting to look like I just got out of the shower. Wow." Like a southerner in a heat wave, she began fanning herself rapidly with her hands. "If I get any hotter, I'm going to have to take my sweater off. I've never stripped in front of a crowd before." Again, the audience broke into huge laughter. What was happening before their eyes was affecting them as well. A kind of excitement filled the air. It was like watching a miracle unfold before you.

"Well, if you want to take your sweater off, I think we can find a sheet or something to hide you. Are you doing OK?"

"Oh my, the dizziness is really getting bad. I hope I don't pass out," she said looking at Michael as if she were a damsel in distress and he were Dudley Doright who could save her.

"I think we'd better get you some water to drink." Turning his focus to the watchers, Michael continued, "It's quite common for the body to give off huge amounts of energy during a session. And that can mean that water is needed to refresh and resaturate the body. The water also acts as a grounding device to help get rid of the dizziness. Oh, good, a nice big bottle of water. Has it been blessed?" The young woman who had handed him the bottle nodded yes. Everyone watched bug-eyed as the lady in orange downed the bottle like a logger guzzling a tankard of beer.

Gary interjected at this point and added, "Michael, would you check to see if her spleen meridian is OK? I'm seeing a blockage there as well."

"Sure, good idea." Michael flipped his laminated card over and started checking meridian paths, the same used by acupuncturists and Chinese medicine practitioners. "Yep, you're right. The spleen meridian is blocked. Do I have your permission to clear your spleen meridian?" he politely asked the lady.

"Honey, you have my permission to do anything you want." Michael laughed along with the audience. Once again he invoked the woman's angels and guides to assist her in this effort. And this time the frivolity changed into high emotion. Within seconds, this affable, delightful matron went from all smiles to exhibiting tears. Obvious emotions erupted on her face as she began to silently weep. Michael asked for tissues. The tender silence changed the conference hall into a sanctuary. Others reached for handkerchiefs as well, dabbing their eyes. Telltale sniffles fractured the quiet in several places.

"God, honey, this is so embarrassing." A lady who wasn't afraid of stripping in front of the gathering now was afraid of exposing herself in another way. How often do we do this to ourselves in American society, where the jester and the tough person are admired, and the tender heart is hidden in shame? How intimate the setting had become. How revealing to everyone. Earlier in the talk, Gary had pronounced to the audience that when we heal one, we heal all. How evident that had become in the time it took a pendulum to swing back and forth. Michael kept checking his reference card.

"No need to be embarrassed. We are all friends here. You've got angels helping you and watching out for you. I see that you are almost done. Almost all the blocks are gone. How do you feel?"

"Darling, I feel great. It's like this huge weight has been lifted from me. I feel so alive. This is great."

"Wonderful. Glad to hear it. OK, I'm getting that everything has been cleared," he said, folding his pendulum into his hand and placing it back into his vest pocket. "I want to you thank you for coming up here and showing everyone how this works. You were wonderful, really wonderful." Orange arms surrounded Michael with gratitude. As this delightful woman returned to her seat, the entire hall erupted in applause. Never had Michael been so appreciated in public, never had he heard the thunder of such recognition. It was now time for questions, and hands shot up like bean sprouts with people wanting to know more about what had just happened.

A younger man wanted to know what it was the lady was experiencing, what it was that made her so hot, what it was that caused the healing. After letting the woman speak from her own perspective, Michael decided to answer the man's question with a story. "First of all, it doesn't matter what someone else does in terms of our own healing. If we are not ready for healing, nothing will work, or if it does, it will only be temporary. We are our own healers. You see that even in ancient texts like the Bible. In there you hear over and over again where Jesus keeps saying, 'I have done nothing.' He meant it. What you just saw was my assisting this lovely lady with her own desire for healing. You know, if we want healing in our lives, we have to be ready for that. We have to allow the healing to occur in our body when someone works with us.

"The reason for the heat comes from two factors. Firstly, I am using what I call grace, or the essence of love, the life force, to help break up miasms or blocks that keep the body from healing itself. Our bodies are tremendous healing machines. It is the rule to be healthy and the exception to be ill. The illness comes out of our inability to let ourselves heal. In this case, I noticed the energy immediately break loose when I worked with grace, asking this lady's angels to assist also. This gateway we stood in is a doorway, an opening to grace. In fact, Gary and I call it the Gate of Grace, which is nothing more than the essence of Divine Love. When the connections between me and the person I am working with are good, heat usually is a sign of the healing starting up. When people start perspiring, as in this case, you know that a lot of work is getting done. And it's a team effort between the person, myself, and the angels. When the heat was gone, that told me that the healing of the physical was complete. But you noticed a lot of emotional energy also release when we dealt with past-life issues. Sometimes we come into this life with baggage from past-life situations. We often move into relationships that have karmic debt or karmic consequences. And if we don't learn from them, or if we don't overcome the karma, we can fall into a diseased condition. People really do get hot from the work, they tingle from the top of their heads to the bottoms of their feet.

"About two months ago, I worked with a woman who watched the swelling in her feet decrease as we were working together. She said, 'My gosh, my feet are getting smaller right before my eyes.' How do you explain a phenomenon like that? Well, this woman was a student of Christian Science for many years. We had worked together off and on for two years. She was quite familiar with my energy and healing ability, and lately the added use of grace. She accepts that a healing is going to happen. She now knows it is going to happen. It's in situations where you have complete acceptance by the person where it really makes a difference. There's nothing in the way of the connection between the healer and the healee, the angelic realm and the person's guides. That's the ideal situation.

"Usually, when healing takes place, it begins first on the etheric level, and then the etheric is transferred to the physical over a matter of days. In this case, and in the case of the lady with the swollen feet, the etheric was transferred to the physical almost immediately. And that's the phenomenon that occurs when you have everything working extremely well. How did I know that our volunteer would be one of these situations? I dowsed asking for someone who was willing, ready, and able to allow healing to occur. My pendulum swung over in the direction of our volunteer when I picked her out of the many who had raised their hands. I want to thank her greatly for giving us such an environment for everyone to learn. Thank you. Thank you very much." He bowed in the direction of the grateful woman.

Even more hands shot up after this answer. People could feel the rightness of what they heard and what they had seen. They were hungry to know more and learn more. These are the days of wonder, and people want to hope in the authenticity of the wonder, trust in the hope that wells up within them. We are a world in need of trusting in our own healing.

An older lady asked, "What happens when folks go back to their doctors after they have had a healing like this?"

Michael chuckled a bit and looked over at Gary. "There are many answers to that question. I worked on a case with Gary where the lady had advanced lupus, which is an incurable disease. Like these other cases, there was a spontaneous healing overnight. She was ready. When she went back to her doctor and asked to be taken off all her lupus medication, he wanted to know what had happened to her. She wouldn't tell him. She had a hard time telling her husband what had happened. A lot of people don't want to be ridiculed for coming to us, letting people know they've been working with the angelic realm. They're afraid of what people will say. But the doctor did ultimately take her off all her lupus medication, and told her whatever she was doing to keep on doing it. We hear that a lot.

"Then there are cases when clients simply will not go to their doctor anymore. The previous case I told you about, the lady with the swollen feet? There's more to her story. Marilyn was actually 73 years old and had been to her doctor often. A couple of years ago she had chronic back pain and went to ask her doctor what he could do. A CAT scan was ordered and a specialist analyzed it. Marilyn told me how solemn-faced he was when he told her that her back was in such terrible shape there was nothing they could do for her. She would suffer from the back pain for the rest of her life. Marilyn was in a living hell and told me she was starting to go out of her mind from the pain. She then went to a chiropractor who gave her the same sentence — pain for the rest of her life. That's when she gave me call, hearing about me from an associate. I treated her over the phone in a similar fashion you saw here today. I keep a gateway in my apartment when I do my work. During the session, Marilyn began to express comfort, telling me that a tingling sensation was traveling up her back, that the pain was subsiding. I worked on her for an hour, checking for other conditions which might have contributed to the pain. Disease can come from any one of our bodies: the physical body, the emotional body, the mental body, or the spiritual body. In Marilyn's case, the relief was immediate, and she has had no recurrence of the pain since that day. Marilyn is the ideal client. Now, the reason I'm telling you this story is that Marilyn won't even go back to her doctor anymore. And I'm not saying that people shouldn't see their doctors. Physicians can often play an important role in our healing process. What I do is no substitute for sound medical treatment. But I do have to admit that I see a lot of people whose doctors have given up on a cure.

"I also hear from people who are told by their doctors that surgery is the only answer. And they want to know what other options are available. I had such a client in Portland, Oregon. A few years ago she started having unbearable leg pains, so bad that she would wake up crying from it. Her legs were so swollen that on some days she wouldn't remove her shoes for fear she couldn't get them back on. Because she had a sensitivity to drugs, also, she decided she needed to find an alternate therapy to her painful condition. When her right leg started dragging from her condition, she went to an orthopedic surgeon. After many tests and x-rays, she was told that her spine looked in such bad condition that it would require surgery. She told the doctor she wouldn't consider surgery as an option. And he told her, 'Then you will have to live with the pain.' That's when she called me. In her case it took a few days before the swelling went down and the pain left. And she hasn't had a leg problem since.

"Recently she called with a slipped disk in her neck, causing her great pain. Once again I worked on her remotely. And because she was now in a more open frame of mind, within thirty minutes the disk eased back into place and the pain left. She tells me that what she likes best about me is my irreverent sense of humor. Never discount the role of humor in helping people to heal."

The questions came in rapid fire as the time began to run out. The Expo facilitator had to give the high sign to close the workshop for the next workshop scheduled in the hall. One last question was taken. "What has changed in your life since you've started doing this kind of work? What has this done for you?"

Not one to talk about himself much, Michael scratched his head, wondering what he should say. A twinkle in his eye betrayed his desire to tell another joke. But because time was short, he simply answered, "Well, it's given me ... it's reinforced my own perspective that there is more to us than what meets the eye. And certainly it reinforces the feeling that we are all interrelated, and that we are all here for reasons. Many times we don't recognize why we are here precisely. But there are reasons. We know we are here to change the energy in the world, we are here to serve others, we are here to help our own Self, own our karma, or to learn our lessons. We are here to deal with our own contracts for acquiring wisdom through our lessons, as well as affecting other people in our lives in positive ways. Abraham Lincoln once said, 'A man is about as happy as he makes up his mind to be,' and my feeling is that it is very important to be happy, because searching for happiness invites us to structure our lives or structure other people's lives in pursuit of that happiness. That's one reason why I tell a lot of jokes. I try to bring happiness to people because if you're laughing it will make your life better in so many ways. Everybody has different things they need to do in their lives and if they can do it with a smile then what they contribute has more power, it allows them to feel empowered. A smile is a powerful tool.

"It's important that we feel empowered. One of the things I like to say about my work is that I try to focus on people's lives working, moving forward. You know, it's not about what I want for them, it's about what is in their highest and best interest. There is a lady that taught about relationships at Unity Church in Portland, where I visited. She said, 'You're in a marriage or a relationship to help the other person to become more of what they can be — not what you want them to be — but more of who they can be.' And that's the thing I try to do when I work with people — just empower them to be more of who they can be rather than what everyone wants them to be. You know every one of us is unique and powerful in that respect."

From past experience, Gary knew he needed to step in and end the workshop. Too many times in the past, in working with Michael, he had found himself leaving a workshop several minutes and even hours after the workshop was over. Michael genuinely loved people, loved to listen to them, loved to help them. However, Gary had also witnessed what happened to Michael afterwards. Some men give so much of themselves that they drain their own energy. And Michael was one who could give until it wiped him out. His past skills as a TM¨ meditation instructor certainly served him in getting his energy levels back up after long sessions. But it was Gary's way to provide an ounce of prevention rather than putting Michael into a position where he, himself, needed a pound of cure.

The relationship between Michael and Gary had grown into one of deep mutual respect. Each had his gifts, his own personal magic that he brought to people. They were a terrific team in workshop situations and also in serving clients. Gary's one impediment, however, was that he would not do remote healing, at which Michael was quite adept. So the time they spent with one another was more rare than either liked. Their friendship was one of mutual support, often to the point where it became instructive in ways neither could understand. Such a time occurred when Gary found himself immersed in a family mess involving real estate inherited from his mother and father. His younger brother had gotten himself in some trouble and was about to lose the property left to the two brothers. Gary had to use legal maneuverings to wrestle the property into his care before it went into receivership. But what he didn't know, with all his traveling and sparse contact, was that the property had fallen into ruin, with his brother illegally logging the trees off for spare cash. By taking control of the property, Gary found himself jumping from the frying pan into the fire. The property would not sell. Even as a fixer-upper it would not sell because of the many liens against his brother.

At the time, Michael knew something was wrong, and asked Gary to confide in him. After relaying the entire story, Michael volunteered to help. "How?" Gary asked. "It hasn't sold for six months. In fact, there hasn't even been a single inquiry for that whole six months. Not one single interested party has come forward. This is a complete mess."

"How about I clear the property of whatever is in the way, whatever it is that is keeping it from being sold?"

"You can do that?"

"Yeah. Fax me a map of the property, signifying true north. Be sure to give the layout of the house and any other significant point on the property. I'll dowse to see what's inhibiting a sale from coming forward."

The map was faxed within the hour. Michael called back with information. "I see what's wrong here. What I'm being told is that your parents gave this to you and your brother as a family legacy. They wanted you both to have something you could be proud of."

Gary responded, "Yes, that's true. I pretty much gave the house to my brother since I would never be there. It's close to a lake, near recreational grounds; it was a great place. I helped build the house myself. I hate seeing what has happened to it."

"Well, there is a lot of anger around the house. Your brother is furious with you and wants you to fail in your efforts. I can ask the angels to move in and protect the property, to move in and clear out all the impediments, and I can ask you to set the intent that whoever buys it will preserve the initial integrity your parents wanted for the property."

"Wow, that sounds great, Michael. Do it."

After about five minutes of silence, while Michael did his thing, the two continued their conversation. "OK, Gary. I've dowsed that it is important that the price of the house end in a number 4. That is your prosperity number. And I've dowsed that the property will sell for $41,800. I know that's low but it's probably the best you'll get in its present condition. You could get a lot more for it if you cleaned it up and do some repairs but you said you didn't want to sink another penny into it. So if you add up $41,800, you'll get 4+1+8, which is 13, which adds up to 4. That's the price."

Three days later, Gary got a phone call from the realtor. A party was interested in buying the house as a fixer-upper but they wanted to do a private contract rather than go through a bank loan. Gary was dumbfounded. The property sold. And the price? $41,800.

This was not the only real estate clearing that Michael had done and it would not be the last. After the Spokane Expo, his reputation spread even more. Phone calls from all around the nation made their way to Victor, Montana, where Michael and Jane live. Their days are dedicated to the helping, healing, and empowering of others. Both are people of the heart, who see the world for what it can become instead of what people make it out to be. Their lives serve not only to better others; their lives serve to remind us all that we have a choice in this world. We can choose to suffer or we can choose to help one another become whole, healing not only ourselves but our world. Remember — when we heal one, we heal all.

Awakenings
Michael Hoefler
P.O. Box 517
Victor - MT 59875
406-642-3630
awakenings1@qwest.net

Harvey Caine
Synergy: Fully Integrated Healthcare
1605 W. Garland, Spokane - WA 99025
509-245-3838.

PART III

CLOSING THE JOURNAL

9

THE SYMPOSIUM

As the popularity of *The Messengers* grew, invitations and inquiries began pouring in. Would Nick speak before our group? Would Nick join our efforts? Can Nick answer this question or that question? Something had to be done to address the groundswell of requests. Brian, Gary, and Nick put their heads together in deciding it was time to create a setting where Nick could present his story, answer questions, and remind people of Jeshua's messages, especially those addressing healing in one's spiritual life. But where to begin? Seattle had been the jump-off point for the book, why not a symposium as well? Though Nick would be the only speaker for this event, a symposium format was designed so that additional speakers could be brought in at future events. It would be a format that would allow a public ministry to grow around Nick as well as those who would embody the ideals found in Jeshua's messages.

Brian set to work getting the right people organized for such an event. The venue would be the Washington State Convention Center in downtown Seattle. Graphics were designed and pictures collected so that an audience could see more clearly what would be presented.

It would be an effort almost as grueling as trying to publish the book. Sound engineers, video engineers, lighting specialists, ushers, ticket collectors, security people, bookstore people, and publicity people all had to be taken care of. Coordination was monumental with the short time available to get everything ready. Brian spent more time on the phone than he did sleeping in bed. The day was growing close and only two-hundred tickets had been sold for a convention ballroom that could hold a thousand. It wasn't that numbers were so important as it was that a good model be created for future events such as this.

In a meeting filled with scratching heads, the question was asked whether the symposium should be canceled. Nick's businesslike determination pointed to trusting that people would show up at the door. Others countered that events such as these only draw 25 percent of their crowd at the door. The other 75 percent comes in advance sales. Nick pointed out that nothing about this project had been done according to the norm. And this would be no exception.

As the Convention Center doors opened, people from as far away as Vancouver, Washington, to Vancouver, Canada, were already waiting. Nick would learn later that well-wishers had come from as far away as Salem, Oregon, to participate in his symposium debut. As the time approached for his introduction, ushers were wondering whether additional chairs would have to be retrieved. Almost a thousand people were present, buzzing with anticipation, as Paul White introduced his friend and colleague, Nick Bunick.

What pleased Brian the most was the mix of friendly people making acquaintances with their neighbors two and three chairs down. It seemed more like a great picnic than a symposium. People from all walks of life had gathered. Men in business suits sat next to men who looked as though they'd taken off a day from working in the woods. Teenagers sat with parents. Seniors using walkers to find aisle seats stared bemusedly at swaying toddlers pulling chew rings and soppy fingers from their mouths. Women in flowing dresses smiled with acknowledgment at others in work clothes. It was a day where the best in people seemed to beam brighter than the ballroom spotlights.

As Nick stepped to the podium, a discernible gleam in his eye seemed to say that this was what it was like 2,000 years ago. As then, people wanted to hear about, to be reminded of the messages with which Jeshua had blessed the world. Opening his binder anxiously, Nick began to speak with a earnestness that stilled the crowd immediately.

"It was 2,000 years ago when Jeshua taught his followers," Nick began. "He told them that every one of us is a child of God — God our Father and Mother. That means that all of us here are brothers and sisters. So I say to you, not condescendingly, but from the heart, good afternoon to you, my brothers and sisters."

Several voices in the crowd returned a soft "Good afternoon." Children waved as if they'd already made a new friend. Others simply said, "Hi." It was the kind of rumble of voices that one heard when a church full of people prayed together. Nick cleared his throat, grabbed a glass of water as he rearranged his notes. His eyes checked the crowd one more time as he tested the remote control unit in his hand and turned a discerning eye to the twelve foot screen behind him.

"Can everyone see the screen OK?" he posed as if asking friends if they could see the football game on TV well enough. "Everyone relax and feel at home. If you feel the need to get up during my talk to take care of yourselves, please feel free to do so. The bathrooms are outside the ballroom doors, down the hallway, and to your right." The excitement was transforming into affection. This would be no ordinary talk. Everyone was at home, only now, home would be in the middle of the Washington State Convention Center.

"This is a very special day for me," Nick continued, "And I hope, for you, also. I'm breaking down this material into three different segments. In the first portion, I want to share with you the events that took place in my life, going back to 1977, so that you can understand the challenges that I went through, the metamorphosis I went through, to have the determination and the commitment to be here today, to accept God's mission. This purpose now remains with me for the rest of my life.

"The second segment will cover events that happened 2,000 years ago. Events that will be given in greater detail than can be found in Scripture — and even, in some places, that conflict with Scripture. I want to share with you why they conflict, and I want to share the experiences I have been exposed to in the memory of Paul so that you can have an understanding of why there were distortions and inconsistencies.

"In the third segment, I'm going to share with you the messages of Jeshua of 2,000 years ago, as well as contemporary messages I feel I have a responsibility in sharing. There are going to be some major events that are going to happen in the world as we move into the new millennium. Let me make it clear that I am not talking about the *end* of the world, but the beginning of a new world.

"I will leave time for questions after our intermission, and then I will move into a transition where I will expose you to what Jeshua taught to the crowds about healing of the spirit."

On the projection screen stood a giant angel with its arm extended as if in invitation. Nick turned, clicked his remote, delivering a large map of Judea, Samaria, and Galilee. In the back of the ballroom, autographing of the book ceased, ushers took seats, all eyes focused in front on the screen and the man who had traveled across 2,000 years to be with them.

As Nick's words related his own journey of what it took to get him to this day, in this ballroom, pictures waltzed across the projector screen, people looked around, and smiles continued as those attending continued to sense something in the air, as if the angels themselves were present. With the first section of the presentation delivered, Nick launched right into the second section.

"There is a spiritual consciousness spreading around this world," his voice insisted, resounding through the sound system. "Not just here in this gathering, not just in Washington, not just in the Pacific Northwest. Not just in our country and not just on our continent, but all across the world. More people between now and the year 2012 will open their hearts and souls to God than ever before in the history of mankind because of the wonderful things that are going to happen in the future. They'll understand the presence of God and God's messengers, and they'll realize the presence of Jeshua and his messages in all our lives.

"All of you came here today using various forms of transportation. Some of you perhaps drove in a car with friends; some of you by public transportation; or maybe some of you even walked. Regardless of how you got here, it is the same with finding God. There are many different ways. Whether you are Christian, Jew, Hindu, Buddhist or Islamic, we are all on the same journey. And that journey is to find God. We are all children of God." Smiles eased across faces at hearing a message that they inherently knew to be true. It was gladsome to have someone who spoke with the authority of Paul the Apostle to say so.

"I'm going to take you back 2,000 years," he continued, "back to the Sea of Galilee, where Jeshua spent most of his childhood in Capernaum, where his family lived. Even though it is mentioned in Scripture that he was from Nazareth, where Mary and Joseph had originated, he actually grew up in Capernaum, in the same region as Nazareth, some 70 miles north of Jerusalem. That is the reason why most of his early disciples came from the Sea of Galilee. Peter and Andrew came from Bethsaida, located on the northern shore. John and James, sons of Zebedee, also came from that area on Galilee's shore. The reason why this particular province is important stems from the fact that it wasn't under Roman occupation; it was not part of the Roman Empire as was Jerusalem and the region of Judea. Galilee's topography and vegetation, then, was not unlike the greenery and rolling hills of this area. Great agricultural and fishing businesses flourished in this area, servicing the larger population of Jerusalem. There was much activity in the area around Galilee which could take place that was not allowed in the area around Jerusalem. And the people were more independent and less pious in the Galilee. The reason they were less pious lay in the area's conquest 200 years prior by the Babylonians and Assyrians. Many of the conquerors had settled down and intermarried with the indigenous population. The intermarriages fostered more religious diversity and less dedication to the Judaic religion adhered to in Jerusalem. So Jeshua found himself in a land that didn't make much of fuss about his own teachings. That's the primary reason for Jeshua's many trips to Jerusalem during his teaching ministry. He had the best of both worlds. The Romans didn't pay much attention to him as a resident of Galilee, yet he could visit Jerusalem to teach and fulfill his ministry."

It was fascinating how much information Nick retained from his memories of Paul. Not only was his understanding of language nuances and cultural subtleties remarkable, but so were detailed descriptions of the terrain, what people ate and wore. It was like being able to take a TV camera back into the ancient past and watch what was happening during the time of Jeshua. Nick continued to paint vivid pictures of the provinces and cultures of what was known as Palestine. Intimate detail of Paul's arrival to the area at the age of eighteen, and his travels through the Holy Land proved fascinating. Nick began to describe the various sects of the region to show people how Paul's own presence as Nick Bunick was possible some 2,000 years later. He touched upon how belief in reincarnation was a part of the Jewish culture, especially with those who belonged to the sect called the Pharisees, of which Paul was a member.

The second section continued with examples from history as to how certain beliefs and biases stemmed from that time. Nick wanted people to understand why there were differences in his memories as Paul and some accounts described in Scripture. Some in the crowd were starting to get a little restless. The history lesson was important to those who wanted verification that Nick was indeed the return of spirit and soul of Paul. Why had he returned? Why was he daring to tell the world that he had a message? Nick noticed the oncoming restlessness. But he felt groundwork had to be laid before he opened the floor to questions. He turned the presentation around, at this point, to reflect why he and this ballroom full of people had come together this day.

Nick continued to describe his present-day journey and how it had paralleled Paul's. This time, instead of Jeshua intervening, angels had intervened in his life. And like then, he once again was telling people about the loving messages he had learned from his beloved friend. Seattle was his present-day Damascus, where he had begun his ministry two millennia ago.

Like the previous gathering in Salem, Oregon, Nick guided his audience through the history and the cultural dialog that had produced concepts like hell and the devil, which really did not exist during Jeshua's time. There had been no Satan with a capital S. The only way Jeshua used such a term was in its cultural roots, where the word connoted not a being, but a state of being. Like the Salem gathering he watched smiles etch across the faces of those gathered as he revealed that the concept of hell had been created from a past that used the notion metaphorically, specifically citing the word "Gehenna," which had been the actual garbage dump for the city of Jerusalem. Sure, it had horrible smells, and, yes, fires burned there as they do today in landfills, but the term was used then to describe the punishment we put ourselves through when we are not in harmony with the God-Within. Jeshua had been adamant about there NOT being a punishing God, but a loving God.

Nick finished with a brief account of how *The Messengers* had managed to go against the odds and become a bestseller in the region. He described how major publishing house was going to be the new publisher and take the book forth nationally as well as internationally. And he reminded the crowd that the title of the book was not simply about angels. It was about all who help to remind the world how we can live in an atmosphere of love, peace, and well-being. All who were in the ballroom were, themselves, messengers. He thanked them for their support, their hope, their love. As the lights hummed to full brightness, a resounding applause filled the great space. It was intermission time, and everyone wanted to hear what the angels had to say about what was to come.

Nick had stated before leaving the stage that questions would be allowed before the beginning of the second half of the afternoon's program. Microphones were set in place as everyone took a break. Rather than return to the green room to rest for the next part of his talk, Nick circled back from behind the stage and shook hands with those who wanted to meet him. The energy in the air was electric, and he felt the need to immerse himself in it.

As the lights dimmed and the chatter of the crowd subsided, Nick returned to the podium ready to field questions. It was time to continue. "We are going to have a question and answer period, now, because once I start my next section, I'm going to want everyone focused and quiet without interruption as I take you through what Jeshua taught me, and that is the healing of one's spirit."

Eyebrows were raised and glances exchanged as pockets of murmuring spread throughout the crowd. It was as if everyone knew they were being awakened to events that had been ancient, even forgotten. This was to be a day of remembering.

As the first questioner grabbed a microphone, everyone settled in for the next phase of the symposium. "You have stated that parts of Scripture have been subject to mistranslation. But what about the letters attributed to you, as Paul? Are they accurate, and did you write them?"

Nick took a drink of water as he gathered his thoughts. "Some twenty-one documents have been attributed to Paul. Those documents are the basis for the twelve letters, or epistles, of Paul found in today's Scriptures. Through my memory as Paul, I am aware that over 100 letters were written during his lifetime." The crowd shuffled in their chairs, all eyes forward. This was just the kind of stuff they'd come to hear. "In reviewing all the documents attributed to Paul, I have come to realize that fourteen of the twenty-one documents, to which biblical scholars refer, had actually been written by Paul.

"I am aware that the Letter to the Hebrews was not written by Paul, that one of the Letters to the Corinthians was actually a combination of several different short letters that Paul had written at that time to the community at Corinth. Also, Paul did not write the Letter to the Ephesians, even though it has been attributed to him. In his later years, Paul's eyesight was failing him, and he could no longer see well enough to write. Keep in mind that writing letters in those days was not like today. There was no e-mail, no ballpoint pens, and no typewriters. In fact, there wasn't even paper as we know it. Oftentimes, writing had to be done by dim light. So it fell to others who were close to Paul to write for him. He would dictate the message and they would write it down for him, or later compose the letter at some future date when there was more time. This process, in and of itself, led to some artistic license on the part of the transcriber. That is the reason why biblical scholars of today realize that some of the writings are not consistent with Paul's style, grammar and word choices. Paul's name was affixed to these letters even though he, himself, did not write them.

"Fourteen of the documents that Paul did write are relatively accurate, although certain errors have been made in translation of words from those times. Some of those errors were certainly honest, a matter of the differences between languages, while others leave one to wonder whether word changes were deliberately made."

Others were beginning to line up behind microphones, for the audience now realized this was a chance to ask questions about a time they had long wanted answers to. A well-dressed, thin lady began asking a question at the same time a gentleman at one of the other microphones began. The crowd laughed gently at the enthusiasm. Nick motioned to the lady.

"It has been said that Paul did not care for women. Yet women seemed to play an important role with Jesus in what has been written in *The Messengers*. In there, it is said that Mary had been taught by the Essenes. How could this be if there were restrictions regarding women participating in activities?"

"A good question," Nick rejoined. "The Dead Sea Scrolls are the foundation of written accounts of the Essenes, as we know them today. However, these Scrolls have not been made public until just recently. The Dead Sea Scrolls were found in the area of Qumran, not far from Jerusalem. At Qumran, women played an important role in the Essene community. It's not true, that you hear stories about women not being allowed to participate in Essene activities, that women didn't have an equal right. For they did. Women played a very, very important part in the Essene way of life. Mary, as a young girl, was taught by the Essenes at Mount Carmel. She underwent training because they thought she was one of a number of young women who they felt could be the vessel of delivery for the coming Master, Jeshua. So, yes, Mount Carmel did exist, though not as well known as Qumran. One of the reasons the Dead Sea Scrolls had been held from the public, rests in the leader of the group in charge of those Scrolls and their translations, a Father DeVault, who recently passed away. The entire team of scholars in charge of the Dead Sea Scrolls, except for one person, came from the clergy. And there are teachings in the Scrolls that cause some concern to certain organized religions. So the Scrolls have been kept from the public until the Huntington Library, in Los Angeles, unilaterally decided to release the microfiche version to the general public. It caused quite a stir.

"But the Essenes did not have disrespect for women. Quite to the contrary, women played a very important role in the community. At Mount Carmel, there was a woman by the name of Judi, who was in charge of the educational system of the community. In other words, she was one of the ruling leaders. She not only was in charge of Mary's education, but years later, was also in charge of teaching her young son, Jeshua.

"Did Paul discriminate against women? The truth is the absolute opposite: Paul had a great respect and love for women. If you read the letters of Paul, the last paragraph of every letter in Scriptures, he is thanking all those who are ministers and helpers of his churches in every place he had written to. In every letter, he mentions almost as many women, if not more, than he does men.

"You must understand, that at that time, women and men had different positions in their society. But at no time did Paul ever discriminate against women. Women played a very important part as *apostulae*, or teachers. They were also ministers in the early Church. But unfortunately, the "old boy" network of the medieval Church didn't want women involved, so they tried to eliminate any knowledge of women having such a prominent role, and that's why they didn't allow women to become priests."

A ruffle of applause moved through the audience as women noted the struggle they had faced throughout history, objects of the patriarchal era of religious history that plagued them to this day. The gentleman who had waited patiently for his turn, waited again as the applause quieted. "How about the issue of Paul establishing a requirement of celibacy among Church leaders? Has that not carried over today into the Catholic and Orthodox religions?"

Nick looked over the gathering of people. His heart went out to them as he realized the centuries of bewilderment and difficulty they had endured because of hierarchical attitudes during the Middle Ages. It troubled him how convenient a vehicle Paul had become in justifying the actions they took, after whole sections of Scripture had been edited, even eliminated. Truly, it was time to set the record straight. Whether present-day religions would acknowledge the truth of what he was about to say was neither here nor there. It had to be said. "The truth is that Paul's position was that one could be a minister of the Church and be married. But only if you had total fidelity to that marriage. He felt it would discredit the ministers as well as the churches and their teachings if these couples were not completely faithful to one another.

"On the other hand, if one was single and wanted to be a minister, Paul wanted that person to be celibate, so that the leaders of the Church would not have affairs with the members of the congregation. As you may recollect in *The Messengers*, this was a problem in the early days of the Church. However, Paul also stated that if you have such a love for a woman, or a man, wanting to have a carnal relationship, then you should proceed in getting married, rather than having the relationship while you were single. Again, he was trying to protect their relationship as well as trying to prevent his ministers from having affairs. He felt such behavior would destroy credibility in the ministry and the teachings in that ministry.

"It was only years later that the medieval Church changed this doctrine, yet justifying those changes by saying that they were trying to follow Paul's instructions. It was they who came up with the idea of men being celibate, and they had reason for this. In those days, the Church had tremendous wealth. It was concerned that if these clerics married and had families, they would leave their wealth to their wives and their children. Therefore, in order to prevent that from happening, they were told they could not marry, so the wealth would remain with the Church when they died. However, it is commonly known that many of the Church leaders had mistresses and were anything but celibate. Keep in mind, also, that many of the clerics of those days were itinerant. They often did not have buildings and communities. It was also easy for anybody to throw on Church garb and proclaim to be a priest so that they would receive food and whatever else they needed in the village they might be visiting. It was a problem for the Church in those days. These itinerant clerics were basically uncontrollable. The Church needed to control these clerics. So the concept of tying clerics to regions was also initiated along with celibacy. Paul was concerned with integrity and Church reputation. The medieval Church was concerned with wealth and power."

"Thank you," said the questioner as the next person stepped up to a microphone. "You say you are the reincarnation of Paul. Yet the Scriptures do not mention reincarnation, and the Churches teach against it. How do you account for this?"

It was a common question Nick had become used to answering during the many radio interviews that had already taken place.

Rather than give a quick answer, Nick decided to go into detail, for he knew that people in the audience had to answer to others who would ask them the same question, whether they were giving the book out as a gift, or whether they would have discussions within their families.

"There were three sects of the Judaic religion. There were the Sadducees, who did not know what happened to the soul or body after death. The Essenes and the Pharisees were the other two sects. Both believed in the soul's ability to return through another body — what we call reincarnation. This belief was the dominant belief among the people of that time. In modern Israel, the opposite is true. The dominant sect then was called the Sadducees. I share this with you because someone might ask, 'How can you stand before me and say that you lived 2,000 years ago if this is in conflict with the teachings of Jeshua, and the teachings of Paul?'

"Paul was educated as a Pharisee, and Jeshua was educated among the Essenes. Both came from religious traditions that believed in reincarnation. Personally, I want to say upfront that it doesn't make a difference whether you believe in a single life or reincarnation. It doesn't make any difference in terms of your relationship to God. All that's important is how you live your life and how you embrace the messages of God, the laws of God. But I do want to share with you what the belief was at that time in history.

"We find in the writings of the great historian, Flavius Josephus, who was born in the year 37 A.D., just a few years after Jeshua was crucified, 'Do you not remember that all pure spirits, when they depart this life, obtain the most holy place in heaven, and they are again sent into pure bodies...?' Also, in his *Antiquity of the Jews*, we find, 'Pharisees believe that their souls, after moral vigor in them and virtue, shall have the power to revive them again.'

"Josephus was a Jew who was captured by the Romans while they were tearing down the city of Jerusalem during the revolt of 70 A.D. Because of his brilliance, they eventually brought him to Rome to serve as a historian. He died in 100 A.D.

"The teachings of the Qabala represented a hidden wisdom behind the Jewish Scriptures of those days. At the same time that the Gospels were being written, Rabbi Simeon ben Joachim wrote, regarding the holy writings of the Zohar, 'All souls are subject to trials of transmigration (or reincarnation) ... for the soul to reenter its absolute substance to accomplish this end. They must develop all the perfections, and if they have not fulfilled this during one life, they must commence another, a third, and so forth, until they have acquired the condition that fits them with their reunion with God.'

"In the writings of another historian, Philo of Alexandria, who was born 20 years before Jeshua and died in 54 A.D., we find, and I quote, 'The air is full of souls. Those that are nearest to earth, descending to be tied to mortal bodies, return to other bodies, designed to live in them.' Prominent Christian leaders such as Justin Martyr, Origen, and St. Gregory talked about reincarnation as part of their teachings. Origen said, 'Every soul comes into this world strengthened by the victories or weakened by the defeats of his previous life.' So these were the teachings of those times.

"In 325 A.D., Constantine was emperor of Rome, and anointed the first pope: Pope Damasus. The first Council of Nicea was called, and they proceeded in hiring a group of scholars to translate the Scriptures, which were then in ancient Latin, into contemporary Latin. So the Scriptures had gone from the spoken word, Aramaic, to ancient Greek, and then translated in ancient Latin, later to be translated again into contemporary Latin. It took these appointed scholars 28 years to translate these Scriptures into contemporary Latin. And in the process, they made a decision to purge everything dealing with reincarnation. The theology of that day was then to endorse the belief that there was only one lifetime on earth. Along with that belief was added the belief of a hell, a punishing God, and a devil who they called 'Satan.' And so it was official church doctrine that the only way to receive salvation was through the Church. It was the only way one could find redemption.

"They made a decision, in their minds, that the way they could control the lives of people was through fear, rather than through the love of God. In doing so, they dramatically changed the teachings, the messages, of Jeshua and Paul. In fact, you can look in Scriptures today and find places they missed purging. Both in Mark and Matthew, the disciples are saying to Jeshua, 'Here is a man who was born blind at birth. Is he born blind at birth for punishment, because of his previous sins?' How could these sins be 'previous,' if not from another life?

"In Matthew, we find Jeshua coming to Caesarea where he says to his disciples, 'Who do you say that I am?' And the disciples say, 'Some say you are the prophet, Jeremiah. And others say you are the prophet, Elijah.' And Jeshua's reply is, 'No. I am not he who was the prophet Elijah. He who was the prophet Elijah has already come, and they have taken his life, just as surely as they will take mine.' And Matthew goes on to say that the disciples knew that he was speaking of John the Baptist.

"There are several other places where the purging was not complete." To some in the audience, this was old news. They had already resolved the issues around recognition of reincarnation. But for others, this was a surprise, perhaps even a disturbing surprise. Nick went on to give more examples in establishing credibility for his account of being able to state that he was, indeed, the return of Paul the Apostle. He cited the Fifth Ecumenical Council and its decrees, in the year 553 A.D., called "The Anathemas," which ordained reincarnation to be heresy. What was also cited was the fact that, then, Pope Vigilius and 42 percent of his bishops had boycotted the Council because it was wrong, stating that the Council could not change the teachings of Jeshua and Paul and all the great teachers that had come after them. Intermittently, Nick would emphasize again that it was not important to believe in reincarnation. It was only important to live good lives, and to hear Jeshua's messages.

"Now, I want to say that I applaud almost all teachings of any Church — of any Church — that shares with its congregations the messages of God that make us a better people and lead us to a better life, closer to God's wishes. The one area I truly feel bad about is where a small percentage of the messages have been distorted. What bothers me is that the Churches choose not to go back and look at history and say that some mistakes were made in the medieval Church 1600 years ago. 'Some mistakes were made. So let us correct them now.'

"But they don't say that, and choose not to change their ways. I am very concerned about that. For I believe in bringing all people together, rather than separating people. But I have been told, 'Nick, your responsibility is to speak the truth as you saw it through the memory of Paul.' So that's what I'm doing."

The audience responded with applause. It was a message that resonated with their souls. Why all this separation? Why can't we come together on the common topic of living lives that strive to connect with God? Nick's eyes twinkled as he looked up. This was his first talk in front of a large crowd. He had endured insults, even attempts at exorcism over the radio airwaves while doing talk show interviews. He had heard all kinds of strange questions and strange logic. But here, he was accepted, he was understood. It was a good feeling.

The next question, like the previous, was another that Nick heard often in his tour across the country. "Why is it in the Gospels that they never mention that Paul and Jeshua knew each other?" Some in the crowd smiled, already knowing the premise to the answer had already been addressed in *The Messengers*.

"Paul was never a disciple of Jeshua's," Nick stated readily. "The word 'disciple' comes from the ancient Latin word *discipulus*, which means 'a pupil.' Paul's relationship with Jeshua was a one-on-one relationship. He was not a pupil, a *discipulus*. And, unlike the disciples, Paul had a higher education, understood the depth of what Jeshua was saying. Oftentimes, the disciples not only had a hard time understanding what Jeshua was saying, but Paul would see them bickering and arguing over their relationship to Jeshua. Those disciples from Judea, the Jerusalem area, such as Matthew and Barnabas were more educated, and less quarrelsome. But Paul really and truly did not care for the disciples at that time. He didn't have much respect for them, and they, in turn, had resentment toward Paul because his relationship with Jeshua was not like theirs. They traveled with Jeshua as a group, while Paul met personally with Jeshua whenever the two of them were in Jerusalem. This resentment became moot when Paul accepted his responsibility after becoming an apostle."

"Could you comment on Scriptures telling us that Paul had persecuted the Christians," the questioner continued.

"This simply is not true for two reasons. Firstly, the word 'criticized' should be substituted for the word 'persecuted.' Whether that translation we have come to read in the Gospels today was a mistranslation or a deliberate slur at Paul is anybody's guess. Secondly, the word 'Christian' did not even exist at this time. There were no Christians at this time. The word wasn't invented until twelve years after Jeshua was crucified. Initially, his followers were called 'The Brotherhood,' or 'The Witnesses.' Paul had no use for this early Church organization, for they were telling people that they had to give up their worldly goods to the Church, or God would punish them if they didn't. This infuriated Paul. Jeshua never had said such a thing. Paul had spoken against this practice, telling The Brotherhood that it was wrong to be telling people this. He reminded them that God does not punish, as Jeshua had taught them. He berated them for frightening people, rather than coming from a place of love, letting well-wishers voluntarily donate their abundance to the cause, instead of threatening with Godly punishment. Paul was also upset because this newfound wealth was attracting freeloaders who were joining the movement simply to share in the communal abundance. This, too, caused Paul to speak with disapproval. 'These are not the teachings of Jeshua,' he would say.

"And that is why Paul did not become an apostle in the beginning. It was actually five years later, while traveling to Damascus, that he experienced a blinding vision. Jeshua appeared to Paul asking him to become an apostle, to help spread Jeshua's messages.

"We are asked to believe that Scripture tells us that Paul was going to Damascus to persecute the Christian Jews there. Now I ask you: Does it makes sense that a Jew from Jerusalem, a citizen of Judea, could go 140 miles through the desert to a foreign country, Syria, and be allowed to persecute people living there who were Syrian citizens? He wouldn't have lasted five minutes before being thrown in prison by Syrian officials. Paul was on his way to Damascus for business reasons. He had a thriving business there which required him to travel back and forth to his businesses in Jerusalem. And finally, it is said that Paul was 'converted,' which simply is not true. He was already a follower of Jeshua's teachings. What he did do was accept Jeshua's request that he himself become a teacher of Jeshua's messages. It was a commitment, not a conversion."

The lines were growing longer around the microphones. It was obvious that many wanted to hear more about what actually happened with Paul and with Jeshua. Nick motioned once again for a question because of competing microphones.

"How did you feel at the time you went public with this controversial information?" a young woman asked. "I understand from your talk that the angels encouraged you. But what was going on within your own mind at that time?"

"I realized that many people might have thought my coming out of the closet with this information was an act of ego. But it wasn't. It was the most humbling experience I ever had in my life. Each morning and night I prayed to God to give me the courage and the confidence to match the commitment I had made. I was concerned about my family having their privacy, about what business colleagues might say, about the consequences I might suffer with the media. Here I was, a high-profile businessman in the Portland area, sitting on the board of directors of a number of corporations, leaving myself open for possible ridicule. It wasn't an easy time. When it came to the media, I simply asked them, even if they chose not to believe what I was sharing with them, to please treat the story with dignity. And they did. I was very grateful. And here I am today."

The next question followed immediately. "Nick, you are using the words 'spirit' and 'soul' to describe your connection with Paul. How do you differentiate the two? Are not they both the same thing?"

"No, I have been shown by Spirit that spirit and soul are not the same. When I speak of the spirit, I am talking about the part of us which God has given as a gift. It is the part of God that is everlasting and immortal. It can never change. On the other hand, our soul is the collection of our personality, intellect, past-life memories, and the values of our spirit. These can change with each human experience we have. As a result of our human behavior, the soul can either create rewards that are due us, or create scars or wounds as a result of action on our part that are in violation of God's messages. That is the primary difference between soul and spirit. Next please."

Pointing at herself to make sure she was next, a older woman asked, "What was it like having your first angelic experience?"

"I was truly in awe," Nick confessed. "I know that it has been explained in detail in our book, *The Messengers*, but there was a part that was left out. At one point, I actually said to the angels, 'I feel so blessed that I am talking to God.' They corrected me and said, 'Not God, Nick, God's guides.' I have come to understand, totally, that angels are truly God's messengers. Every single person has angels in their lives. It is one of the gifts that God gave us. From the day we are born, we have an angel who is assigned to us, who is with us, even until the time when our spirit and soul leaves our body. At different times in our lives, as our own needs change, other angels will come into our lives to help us through different experiences. Angels give us hope when we need hope. They give us inspiration when we need inspiration. Most people are not aware that angels are in their lives, but they are there, if only people would open up to them, acknowledge them, and ultimately recognize them."

"Yes," he said pointing to the same lady who was indicating she had a follow-up question.

"But do you believe that everyone can have angelic experiences?" The 444 stories that were now coming forth from different parts of the country was causing this topic to be one of the most discussed. Questions paraded across the Internet and into the offices. Consciousness about the angels was growing steadily.

"I know without any question, with all my heart and soul, that everyone of us can get in touch with our angels. It is as if you had a radio in front of you, but the button is at the 'Off' position. You must turn the button to the 'On' position, and then search to find the right station. It may not happen the first time, it may not happen the first 50 times you try, but you have only to open your hearts in order for them to communicate with you. But what is most important, you must invite them in, you must believe they can and will help you, beyond any doubt in your mind. They love you, they are with you to serve you.

"Some people have closed their minds and hearts to the fact that the angels are in our lives, and that is very, very unfortunate. On a number of occasions, as I have done radio talk shows around the country, I have had individuals call me who are angry and upset. They tell me there is some passage in the Bible telling us that we are not supposed to pray to angels, and they accuse me of blasphemy for implying that I am praying to angels. Well, my heart goes out to those people. First of all, I know of no such passage in the Bible, and I truly don't care. I don't know when it was written or if it was written. For them to take any passage out of context, even if perhaps it might have been written by Paul 2,000 years ago, is totally wrong and irrelevant.

"There are many passages in the Bible referring to the importance of angels in our lives. But even that is not as relevant to me as to what is happening today. We are truly in an age of miracles. God is intervening in our lives more than ever before. I feel a great sorrow for those people whose hearts and minds are closed because they find one sentence among the many thousands of words in the Bible that they choose to see in a fearful way. Why not focus on the passage, 'Where there is fear, there is not love.' Or perhaps the passage that states that 'God is love, he who abides in love, abides in God, and God in him.' "

Many more questions were asked and answered. Truly there was a hunger in the land for what Nick had to share. It was as if people were being given permission to live their spiritual lives the way they felt they needed to be lived. The evening was wearing on, and the lines to the microphones growing no shorter. Eventually, Paul White had to give Nick the high sign to move on to the next part of the program. "OK, we have time for one last question," Nick said.

"Can you tell us what Jeshua looked like?" was the last question. Of all the questions that Nick heard throughout his travels, this was the most asked question. It inevitably brought a smile to his lips. People wanted to have that connection to Jeshua through him. It was a connection he was glad to provide them.

"I have been sent renderings from others who felt they knew what the face of Jesus was like," Nick offered. "In one set of material, the artist describing her work mentioned that she had taken the liberty of making Jeshua a little huskier because he had been a carpenter. There is a word that was used in an ancient language to describe Jeshua, and that word was 'naggar.' This word can be interpreted in English either as a holy man, a wise man, or a craftsman. Was Jeshua a holy man? Yes. Was he a wise man? Yes. Somewhere along the line, someone chose to take the word 'naggar' and interpret it as 'a craftsman,' which then made him into a carpenter. Now it doesn't really make a difference. Jeshua was who he was whether he was a carpenter or a fisherman or a holy man. But he was not a carpenter. He was thinner than people tend to think of him, because he traveled great lengths on foot. So he was wiry, muscular but wiry. He had the most peaceful expression on his face that made you feel like you never wanted to leave him. His eyes were penetrating, a beautiful blue. Some people say he had dark skin, others say he had in-between skin. The truth of the matter is that Jeshua was from the house of David, as were his parents. In Israel, today, you find all kinds of different colored people. The same was true then. Those from the house of David were mostly fair skinned, as was Jeshua. His hair fell down to his shoulders. His hair was light colored as well, a light brownish with highlights of gold from the sun. He was a handsome man.

"Because so many have asked what he looked like, I have commissioned an artist to do a portrait of Jeshua based upon my memories as Paul. You will be able to see that picture shortly, and we will make unlimited reproductions. I have been told by those who have seen the sketches and the artwork that it is absolutely stunning. You will have to make up your own mind. It is my legacy to the world, from the memory of Paul. I hope you will cherish it as much as Paul cherished Jeshua's love and friendship."

At this point in the symposium, Nick asked for no more questions. With his notes in front of him and projection screen darkened, he took a moment to gather himself in prayer. He then asked those in the audience not to move around during this part of his presentation, for he was going to share with them what Jeshua had shared with him, as Paul, 2,000 years ago: how to call forth a healing of one's spirit. All movement ceased. Everyone in the ballroom sensed the emotion of the moment. They seemed to understand that they were privy to a forgotten time when people had walked with Jeshua. Before them was a man who remembered that moment, remembered those days. And he was about to share all that like no one else in our time has ever shared.

The symposium would change the hearts and even the lives of many. Nick's presentation was more than professional, it exuded authenticity. Later on, television interviews with some of those who had attended the symposium struck those watching their TV screens at home. To hear a woman candidly describe how she had experienced a healing she never thought possible, and then to respond lovingly and convincingly to skeptical questions from the reporter, started a stir in the Northwest that would not be stopped. Sales of *The Messenger* catapulted, setting off a sequence of events that even Nick could not have expected. But where the light burns brightly in the night, the flutter of moths can be heard. And in spite of the outpouring of goodwill and compassion, the moths of night began their flight toward the fledgling Great Tomorrow.

10

VISITORS IN BLACK

With a jolt Gary bolted upright in bed, gasping for air as if reliving his drowning experience from childhood. His eyes searched the river of knotted sheets at his feet as if hoping to find some answer to the question swirling in his head. With its red LEDs, the clock radio on the nightstand signaled 4:44 am. How could he find a way to warn Nick? How could Nick possibly understand what had just transpired in his dream?

Gary worked with the dream world in ways few realize. He had studied with some of the best who know about the Aboriginal Dreamtime and the Way of Wyrd. Himself part Native American, he knew well the legends of the dreamspeakers, those who could move in and out of dreams bringing their messages to those who found their dreams mysterious. Many considered Gary a gifted dreamspeaker with his ability to "become" the dream, rather than interpret the dream. What had just awakened him was no ordinary dream. He knew that from the vividness of the colors, the powerful feelings that haunted him even now, that Nick must be told.

That morning, in the offices of the Great Tomorrow, Gary sat slumped in Beth's guest chair. Beth would understand, perhaps even

177

offer advice. Her wisdom had served Nick well was as executive assistant. Beth and Nick were like bread and butter, though at times one might wonder which was the bread and which was the butter. After much hemming and hawing, Gary unloaded on Beth what had hit him at 4:44 that morning. After listening with the attention of a safecracker, she ordered him into Nick's office where the two men now sat facing one another.

"Mad Dog, you look like man with something on his mind."

"Kinda." He paused, wondering what words would make him sound less like an idiot. "Nick, I've had a power dream. I don't have these very often, but when I do I pay close attention. Last night I had a power dream about you."

"Really? And what was this dream about?"

The words in Gary's mouth felt like marbles. Finally, his spit them out, "The dream was a warning. In the dream I saw you in London."

Nick interrupted in his typical hard-pressing way. "What time period?"

"Well, uh, it felt like the near future. I can usually tell the time of such premonitions by the distance the images are from me or whether they're clear or fuzzy. And the images were in the near-distance rather than the far-distance. So this isn't that far away. While you were in London you were eating at a restaurant with associates. So this tells me that you were engaging in support of these men. Food in a dream usually means some kind of fostering or nourishing of the soul or the person involved in the event. The restaurant table then turned into your office desk and you were writing checks. Behind I could see this shadow figure looking over your shoulder. But the shadow wasn't in your office, it was still in London. The feelings coming off the shadow figure were ominous. Nick, there is a shadow figure in London, and I think he means to do you ill; I think he is trying to sabotage your efforts." There. He'd said it.

Nick rocked silently in his executive chair, the black leather squeaking in cadence to his thoughts. A full minute passed as Nick pondered what had just been presented. Sometimes Gary could be a bit histrionic — a real worry wart. But sometimes he made uncanny predictions about the success of an ad or an event or a person wanting Nick's attention. Nick's fingers gripped the side of his head as he finally rotated the chair around. "It's been taken care of."

"Are you sure? I wouldn't have had this dream if it had."

"Don't worry about it, I know who you're talking about, and the shadow figure has been removed."

Gary sat there dumbfounded. Just as he was about to leave, he heard a commotion outside of the windows of the second-story office. Two crows cawed like crazy, swirling around each other, flying in wild-patterned circles and dives. Then, like a scene out of Hitchcock's *The Birds*, the two crows dove at Nick's office window and began pecking at the window in castanet style. Wings flapped frantically as the two black visitors continued their cawing and pecking on the window. Gary had seen birds fly up to a window for brief seconds, but these two seemed unceasing in their efforts. It was as if they were waiting for some kind of signal to end their ruckus. Gary turned his attention to Nick, wanting to see if his friend would catch a hint from the sight before them. Nick's only response was, "What do you make of that?"

Gary returned his gaze to the two black crows still scrambling against the window. "Well," he started out, "in shamanism the crow is the one of the sacred messengers. Maybe they are here to bring a message. Maybe they are here to enforce the message I brought you about the shadow figure in London." At that point the birds abruptly abandoned their demonstration and flew off.

Nick turned to Gary. "Everything in London has been taken care of," Nick stated in a way that meant the topic was closed. Gary arose with a heavy sigh and left the office, shaking his head on the way out.

In the months that followed, Nick would turn the tables and warn Gary that he was being used by a man with a message, courting his favor. But Gary would not listen to Nick's admonitions. How could this man with such a heavenly message be capable of using others? What irony that both of these men would try to rescue the other while neither would listen to the other, only to suffer the same fate. Even Atira would try on more than one occasion to warn both Gary and Nick of shady situations, only to be dismissed in her efforts. The two crows attacking Nick's office window, as it would turn out, symbolized the fate of both men. For Nick would suffer betrayal at the hands of a shadow figure in London, putting him and his dreams at threat while Gary would suffer disillusionment over being used by a man he thought was his friend. What is it about betrayal that allows it to perform such an important role in life? Poets and philosophers have called betrayal "the great teacher," while others have called it "the kiss of Judas." But without Judas would there have been the Resurrection? Before telling Judas, "Be quick about your business," did not Jeshua say, "I know the kind of men I chose. My purpose here is the fulfillment of the Scripture." When it comes to the purposes of the angels, who knows what is meant to be fulfilled?

In the years that followed, both Nick and Gary would attempt to sift through the ashes of their betrayals. And like the proverbial phoenix rising from the ashes, each would find his new destiny in the children of this world. Nick would involve himself in a program called Child Help USA, started by two amazing women, Yvonne Fedderson and Sara O'Meara. Both women had been childhood celebrities from the "Father Knows Best" TV series of the '50s. And both would join forces in creating an organization after the Vietnam War that would airlift orphans of American servicemen with Asian girlfriends to the United States. Eventually, many orphanages were set up in Asia to address the woes of other children. Their work caught the eye of the U.S. government, which asked them if they could do something for American children. And thus, Childhelp USA was founded. With the help of Merv Griffin, a dude ranch was converted into a village in the Phoenix area where orphaned children could heal emotionally and physically. Presently there are orphanages all around the United States. Recovery programs for abused and battered children have allowed the foundation to take responsibility for these kids, permanently removing them from their parents while they heal. Once recovery is completed, Childhelp USA then proceeds either to find adoptive families or to place the kids in competent foster care programs.

Nick became involved with Childhelp USA after Yvonee and Sara learned about the efforts of The Great Tomorrow also to assist children. In December of 2001, Sara, Yvonne, and Nick, along with members of the staff, attended a formal function in Washington,

D.C., in which Sara and Yvonne received a Lifetime Achievement Award from the President and First Lady. Childhelp USA was honored as one of the outstanding humanitarian foundations in the United States.

Gary, like Nick, later found himself also working with children in ways he never suspected. Unlike Nick's humanitarian programs in The Great Tomorrow, Gary one day found himself incidentally talking before children who were very gifted, what some call "Indigo Children." They, in turn, had questions of him, which caused him to begin thinking differently about his world and about his past lessons stemming from betrayal. In his own quiet way, he began to give some of these kids a voice in how to change our world, bringing them before small groups of people, one city at a time. Modest as his efforts were, such small beginnings are like the planting of a mustard seed: Who knows how big the tree will grow?

No matter which way you look at it, the vision of a great tomorrow looms before us. The lessons that Nick and Gary faced, wrestled with, and eventually overcame, are now being passed on to the youth who come into their lives. As long as there is hope, no darkness can quench the light that comes with a single child entering our world. It is these healed and gifted children who will carry the light of a great tomorrow before us. As Tennyson put it, "The child is the father of the man."

11

The Great Return

From the very beginning, Nick had been told by the angels that he was just one of many sources of light shining throughout the world. Julia had already been aware of this notion. The past-life regressions that Nick and Julia conveyed in *The Messengers* portrayed a world, 2,000 years ago, in the midst of change, especially spiritual change. After Jeshua's crucifixion, Saul, who would later be called "Paul," became a guiding force in the formation of what eventually would be called Christianity. One of the questions asked most often of Nick is, "Why have you returned?" And "Are there others, besides you, who are here from that time?" As in those days, when Paul walked with the Master, Nick finds himself in a world captured in the midst of change.

Traveling throughout the country speaking before people, Nick witnessed repeated incidents accentuating the angelic message that others also would be bringing forth the Light. Letters began arriving from readers who felt they, also, had memories reflecting back to the time of Jeshua. Other letters confessed to a strong feeling that many from that time were here. One letter addressing Nick's not being alone in his journey came from a sports photographer living in San Diego.

May 31, 1997

Dear Nick,

A little less than two months ago, my wife's best friend told her she was sending a book I might enjoy reading. I am a 46-year-old freelance photographer, and just returned from assignment photographing professional spring-training baseball in Arizona. While in Arizona, I had some camera gear stolen the first night, and two days later I was in an auto accident.

My spirits weren't exactly soaring at the time. One day, I noticed a book sitting by our bed. It was *The Messengers*. I asked my wife if that was the book her friend had told her about. She said "Yes." I picked it up and didn't put it down for 24 hours, except to sleep. Mind you, I have never read a book in 24 hours. I am not religious by any means but was consumed by this book. And it has been in my thoughts daily since I read it!

I was raised a Catholic by my parents, but at age eight or nine I decided that going to church was not for me. In later years, I questioned a few things I had learned in catechism ... mainly the statement "God is Love." I couldn't understand how, or why, babies would be born deformed or with deadly diseases, or why good people would die when murderers would live, if God loved everyone. I believed in the basic teachings of Jesus — be good to your fellow man, etc. — and was raised in that manner. Now, thanks to *Messengers*, I understand! In fact, I seem to understand so well it stuns me. I was especially struck by the passage in chapter seven where you write in your journal, and don't remember writing it, realizing the next day it was a message from the angels to you. I still read this passage about courage and integrity frequently, and it is like I'm reading it for the first time.

I'm usually the guy that needs to "see to believe," but now I feel — I KNOW — God's Love, and why things are the way they are. Which brings me to my next point: the auto accident I was recently in.

I was outside Tucson, Arizona — a passenger in a car which was hit by another car going about 45 mph. That car hit about one foot behind where I was sitting in the front passenger seat. It was like an explosion next to me. Yet, after crawling out of the totaled car, I walked away from the accident. Other than cuts on my face and a bloody nose (I think I punched myself when the air bag went off), I was fine. What I remember most is feeling "protected" ... like something was surrounding me. I can't say if the air bag made me feel that way, but I feel more like something was protecting me, shielding me from harm.

Even though I have questioned God — up until now — I have believed in angels (go figure?). I have never seen one, and I can't say why I believe, but I do. Later that evening, my friend — who was driving, and also was not hurt — and I were waiting for a ride in the Park watching a full moon rise over thousands of cactus. I told him I felt we were protected that day by angels. I've never said that to anyone; and that's before I read *The Messengers*!

Since reading *Messengers*, I have had a reading by a woman in Richmond, California, who can also "see" past lives (I'm still working on understanding this). She saw me in a temple, wearing a robe with a turban-type thing on my head. She said I was a teacher-healer, like an apostle, and I have done this in many lives. Which (I think I'm getting near the end here) brings me to my most current experience.

I have just finished *Messengers* for the second time, once again reading it in 24 hours. I was driving to Los Angeles for an assignment to photograph the Braves-Dodgers game. While driving, I was thinking of something you said in the book; that there was a code within. As I was thinking of that, suddenly the words, "They're all here" boomed in my head. I said, "What?" to myself, and the words boomed again, "They're all here!" I mentioned that I have been thinking a lot about *Messengers*, and occasionally I hear things in my head, and I'm not sure if it is just me talking to myself or what. But this was totally different.
My wife, yourself, and others have said something big is going to happen. This may not be anything new to you (of course you have inside help), but it tells me, through what I heard, that all the "players" are definitely on this planet. I seem to know this as sure as I'm typing it.

I totally agree with you, Nick, that this planet is in need of healing. I feel women are going to play a great part in this. The healing, through the power of Love that God has blessed us with, has started. I anxiously await your next book, and I'm very interested in The Great Tomorrow and any seminars you may have. If I can help in any way, I am more than willing!

Thank you, Nick ... no, bless your heart ... for *The Messengers*. All my questions are now answered. One-stop shopping ... gotta love it!!

I hope to hear from you soon. The very best to you and yours.

Kirk

Kirk's comment, "I anxiously await your next book, and I'm very interested in The Great Tomorrow ..." echoed the sentiment of many readers. In collecting material for the next book, Nick asked Julia Ingram, the hypnotherapist who had helped him access his memories as Paul, as well as co-author *The Messengers*, again to regress him using hypnosis. The intention, this time, was not only to interview him through the mind of Paul, but to go into even higher realms to spirit-mind, what some call the "oversoul." Julia explained the concept to Nick thusly:

"I think of my body, or yours, or anyone's, as an energetic container. The body does not even begin to contain all of who we are. We are, at the most basic level, a spirit inhabiting a body. In this body we are a personality. Even more, we are a soul, a composite of all the personalities we have been or shall be; but, even more than that, we are spirit-mind, which extends even beyond what we know as ourselves, which connects with all of life, all of consciousness. And within all of that is what we recognize as our present personality."

As before, Nick regressed easily back to the time of the Apostles. We find Paul in his later years, in his sixties, resting in his favorite spot — his garden.

Julia (J):   Are you indoors or outdoors today?

Paul (P):   I am outdoors, sitting in my yard

J: Are you alone today or do you have company?

P: By myself, right now. [Nick's face has taken on the look of a man several years his senior. Paul's voice was slower in cadence than Nick's normally is. One is left with the impression of visiting a retired, gentle grandfather who has lived much of life. His conversation is that of an old man remembering his past days with fondness.]

J: It's very nice to meet you again, Paul.

P: Thank you.

J: Are you in the mood to have a conversation today?

P: Surely. [He seems surprised by the question. Julia is aware that Paul enjoyed many visitors at his villa where he is essentially under what our culture would term "house arrest."]

Kirk had reflected in his letter what many in our culture are waking up to, when he said, "I totally agree with you, Nick, that this planet is in need of healing. I feel women are going to play a great part in this. The healing, through the power of love that God has blessed us with has already started." Julia wondered if the women who were a part of Jeshua's life had played a role in the conception of the early Church. She was particularly interested in learning if Mary, the mother of Jeshua, had been involved.

J: One of the questions I have for you has to do with Jeshua's mother, Mary. ["Jeshua" is what Paul called Jesus. The word "Jesus" is the Greek translation of Jeshua.] We know that you visited her home and that she came to Bethany from time to time. Could you tell us more about her? What was she like?

P: Mary settled in Bethany after Jeshua left us. For quite a while, her son and daughter were living there with her. Her son, James, moved there. She was a very, very sweet, loving woman. Gentle and quiet and very understanding. And wise in her own little way.

J: Jeshua's death must have been hard on everybody. How did she handle her grief? Did you notice?

P: She was in total pain, and she was hurt. It took her quite a while to make the adjustments. I didn't come in contact with her that often. But when I did, I could see her pain.

J: After you joined the movement, did you have more interaction with her? Did the women participate?

P: Participate in what?

J: Let me ask the question differently. Was Mary consulted about things? Did people ask "Would Jeshua have wanted this?" Or, "Do you think that's what Jeshua meant?" Anything like that?

P: No. She was consulted regarding his death — where to take his body. But I don't recall her being consulted on any decisions that were made with the *apostuli*, the apostles, when they formed the brotherhood. Nor was she consulted about their activities afterwards.

J: How soon was it that James was made the figurehead, if you will? Do you know? [Julia knows about James from regression information described in *The Messengers*. She is aware of the role of James, based upon what she had learned from the history of the early Church, through Paul.]

P: Yes, I know. Cephas [Peter's original name] was actually in charge at first, along with Stephen and Lucius. Lucius became the records keeper, and Stephen was the treasurer. They brought James in originally just to give additional credibility to what they were doing, since he was Jeshua's younger brother. He was a quiet man, unassuming, but very bright. And he took on more and more responsibilities after the first year (after the Crucifixion), and became the figurehead leader. But in a sense, he never had full agreement with the other apostles regarding some of the direction that the brotherhood was going.

J: In fact, he was sort of an antagonist about it in the beginning. I remember your saying that he was even critical of Jeshua.

P: Oh, you're going back.

J: Well, yes, way back.

P: Yes. Yes. He was not supportive when the family was living in Capernaum. He was not supportive of Jeshua. But he accepted Jeshua's teachings and ministries towards the last two years or so of Jeshua's life on earth. He was uncompromising on a number of things. He never, never did agree with the others that we could bring Jeshua to the pagans and heathens. He always insisted, even to the day he died, that you must be Judaic and convert, accepting Judaism, in order to have Jeshua as your guide to God.

J: More aligned with your position?

P: Well, I compromised my position. He never did. He went off on a tangent with a group called the "Ebionites."

J: Could you say more about the Ebionites?

P: Well, they were basically committed to having the Judaic law as your basis for becoming what we called "the brotherhood," which eventually became the "Christians." This happened almost twelve years after Jeshua passed away, left us. In Antioch, the name "Christians" was adopted to identify those who accepted Jeshua as the Messiah. There were several splinter groups, and one of the groups was lead by James. That group splintered away from the rest of us when they chose to go in a different direction, in terms of teachings.

History tells us that the Ebionites (a Hebrew word meaning "poor men") were ultraconservative Jewish members of the early church. Irenaeus tells us that the Ebionites believed that Christ was a divinely endowed man, and that Paul was an apostate from the Mosaic law. Hippolytus and Origen divided the Ebionites into two classes: those that accepted the notion of a virgin birth and those that didn't. But both factions rejected the epistles of Paul. Epiphanius reveals to us that the Ebionites and the faction known as "The Nazarenes," were one and the same.

J: What were the other splinter groups?

P: Well, they had different names, but the primary one of course was the one lead by Cephas [Peter] and myself. The other James [known in history as James the Greater, son of Zebedee], as well as others accepted the compromises. They started out with 70 apostles after they organized themselves after Jeshua died. They took the number 70 from a similar number of members in the Sanhedrin. And as some of them traveled in their missions, converting people to accept Jeshua, they would take slightly different directions and tacks in their teachings. Cephas taught as he wanted to teach, which was different than how I taught. And Apollos, Titus, and others taught others in their own way. That was always a constant challenge. Since there would be more than one missionary that would go through a region, people got exposed to teachings from different missionaries using different tacks.

J: Yes. Was there anything else different about the way James was teaching to his faction?

P: He relied very heavily on Judaic law. He taught more as an intellectual than one who would teach from the heart. I didn't have a lot of contact with him. I primarily got to know him after one of my journeys when I came back to Jerusalem, and stayed for almost three years. [James, Jeshua's brother, was also known as James of Jerusalem.] I tried to make decisions as to how we were going to proceed in reference to the pagans' accepting Jeshua.

J: I'm curious about Bartholomew and Thomas and that group. Was that yet another splinter group, or were they more aligned with already established groups?

P: No. They were fine. They supported us with the majority of people, with what the apostles wanted to do. I relied very heavily on Silas and Timothy those last several years of my journeys.

J: Good allies?

P: Well, we'd go into an area and, more or less, I would try to break through to develop acceptance and create interest. Then I would have Silas and Timothy join me as we did in Athens, then as we did in Corinth. And I would leave them there. I would leave them there and go on to the next place in my journeys. Then I would call for them in the next place I went, have them join me. It was very important that, once we had a fairly good number of people accept our teachings, I would move on and Timothy and Silas would appoint the ministers and leaders of the new church. They might stay for six months or a year until I called them again to the next place. And we would then do the same thing. I would use Timothy, also, to take my letters to other places. There was an imperial postal system that was created by Augustus, but I didn't want to rely on that. So, many times I would have Timothy take important messages for me — letters I had written — to other places. Eventually, I had him stay in Ephesus and settle there to administrate the church.

J: And that's where he remained?

P: Well, he used to come to Rome to visit me. I wanted to see him my last time before I passed away in Rome. For I knew

I didn't have a long time left in my body. [Notice how Paul is talking in the past tense of his death. Julia notices this. It is what she was referring to earlier about having access to the greater consciousness of the soul-mind. Her word for this is the "oversoul." Paul has "drifted" into his oversoul consciousness.]

J: Could you please return to the time when Timothy came to see you in Rome?

P: Yes. He brought Mark with him. And he brought a number of different writings I had left behind. He also brought my favorite cloak I had left behind.

J: You had left that in Ephesus?

P: No. Troas. I had asked them to deliver that for me.

J: How long has it been since you've seen each other?

P: It's been several months, but we communicate.

J: What are his responsibilities, now?

P: He's the chief administrator in Ephesus, and he has help from others. [Historians have given Timothy the title "Bishop of Ephesus" but it appears that no such religious title existed in Paul's time.] I'm trying to encourage him to handle the different factions: the wealthy, the poor, and the merchants, for there are many factions in Ephesus. Every area has its own problems rather unique to their area. I'm trying to help Timothy learn to handle the different personalities. He doesn't like to alienate people or have confrontations, so I have to encourage him to be stronger in terms of making his opinions and his positions felt.

J: He has a softer personality than yours?

P: Well, I don't know if it's softer than mine. I don't want to evaluate my personality. But Timothy is a very gentle soul, very loving, and I encourage him, at times, to be stronger and to be more demanding. Sometimes he doesn't express himself when he feels he might be imposing on somebody.

J: Was there anyone else who would come and visit like Timothy did?

P: At different times, different people. But Timothy was very special to me. Luke spent a lot of time with me, also, when I was in Rome. So, Luke was there a lot, but he wasn't traveling. He was a Greek, and he didn't have the Judaic law background. Silas also spent time with me. I'd say Timothy was my most important visitor, most important companion, and the one I developed a special fondness for. He is much younger than I am.

J: It sounds like you two were very close.

P: Yes. And there were times when I feel like I might get close to Mark. Mark disappointed me when he was younger. Although we became close again, later on, when years went by and he had matured more.

J: You mentioned that Timothy brought you some papers along with your cloak. Were there any personal messages from anyone else, say, for instance, Mary?

P: You mean Mary, Jeshua's mother?

J: Yes, did she write you? Or did Timothy bring you a message from her?

P: No. At this point, Mary had passed on. She passed away in Ephesus. She had moved there after we had established a church community there. She was very close to Timothy. He watched over her the last couple of years.

J: So, she moved from Bethany to Ephesus?

P: Yes, along with Jeshua's sister and another young lady who was a caretaker.

J: Who was that? Do you remember her name?

P: I don't remember, but she wasn't from Jerusalem. She was actually introduced to Mary by Timothy's mother, Eunice. I don't remember her name. Timothy was Greek. His mother Eunice and his grandmother, Lois, were very devoted. They had accepted Jeshua. And Timothy was close to his mother, Eunice.

J: Was John in Ephesus as well?

P: John? Which John? Are you talking about Zebedee's son? One of the followers of Jeshua?

J: Yes.

P: John traveled to different places. He was very, very active, as I was.

J: So he would be in Ephesus from time to time?

P: Well, probably at one time or another they all were. Many of the different teachers (apostles) passed through Ephesus. John was more active in other parts, other regions. He was one of the leading teachers. He spent some time in Ephesus, though, yes.

J: Did Mary every try to contact you while you were in Rome?

P: I didn't have a very close relationship to Mary. When she came to Jerusalem, before I was an apostle, I wasn't involved very much with those other people who were with Jeshua. And I got to know Mary after my experience on my way to Damascus, when I became one of them. I stayed in Jerusalem for several years before I started traveling, and it was during that period that I saw Mary several times. I was never very close to Mary. I had no occasion to get close to her.

J: What you're saying is that she didn't attempt to contact you personally?

P: She would send me greetings through other people, and words of encouragement. Things of that nature. But she didn't try to give me advice to my knowledge. She was a very sweet lady. There was something very special about her. I wish I had spent more time with her.

J: Did you get to know her daughter, Ruth? [Julia knows this name from *The Messengers* information.]

P: Well, not as well as I knew Mary. I probably knew Ruth a little less. She was a sweet young lady. Ruth was heavier in her body than Mary was. She always had a smile on her face, very upbeat personality. Where Mary was more serious.

J: Could you tell us anything you may have heard about the early Essene community before Jeshua was born, and if Mary was a part of that?

P: Yes. There were two Essene communities that I am aware of. One was called Qumran, and it was a little more than a half day's walk from Jerusalem — going towards the Jordan River. The other one was along the Great Sea [Mediterranean Sea] at Mount Carmel in the province of Samaria. When

Mary was a child growing up in Nazareth, she spent, I'm told, a lot of time with the Essenes at Mount Carmel from the time she was a little child.

J: Was she treated any differently from the other children, or was she considered special among any of the others?

P: I wouldn't know that. Although I know she was a very special person. But I'm told that her training was very important. It had a major influence on Jeshua because of her teaching him when he was younger, before he went to Alexandria, in Egypt.

J: You mentioned that Luke visited you often. What were some of the reasons for his visits?

P: I think Luke was fascinated by what had happened, and became very devoted to the teachings of Jeshua through me. He didn't understand. He had a dislike for the Judaic Christians, which bothered me. And I tried to temper that.

J: How would he express his dislike?

P: His background and demeanor was partial towards the gentile Christians, and he felt that the teachings of Jeshua should be accepted and practiced as the gentile Christians were doing it, because the Judaic Christians were involving the Judaic laws and background. Since he didn't have that background, he couldn't identify with it, and thought of them as adversaries of the gentile Christians, which, of course, they were not in most cases. In some places they were, but not in most cases.

J: It is said that Luke was a physician. Is that true?

P: He had medical training, yes. He had practiced as a physician for several years. When he was with me, he was always diagnosing my body. (Paul is laughing.)

J: What kinds of diagnoses?

P: Oh, I was having difficulty with my eyes. He was always criticizing me for not eating, or the way I ate. I was very physically active until those last several years in Caesarea, and then in Rome. My body started to fail me when I no longer journeyed.

J: Were you aware whether Luke did any writing in Rome?

P: He wrote to his family. What kind of writing are you talking about? He didn't write books, to my knowledge.

J: And you don't know if he wrote to any of the other apostles?

P: He wasn't close to the other apostles. Again, they were Judaic, most of them, and he was not. I know he would constantly ask many, many questions when he was around me. He would write notes down of many of those conversations, if that's what you mean by writing.

J: What kinds of questions did he like to ask, in particular?

P: He seemed fascinated with the history of my activities after the Damascus incident. He would ask many questions about that point and on. But then, when he would repeat the answers to me later on, I would have to go over them again because he had a tendency to slant them. He had his own perspective of what he wanted them to mean, sometimes. So I would have to correct this.

J: Did this happen often?

P: It happened often. I felt he had some animosity towards the Judaic people, which I felt was inappropriate. But again, he wasn't there. He came from a different culture, so, I guess that was his slant on things. He had difficulty being objective about it.

Of the four Gospel writers, three embraced the Jewish faith — Matthew, Mark, and John. Only John and Matthew had been disciples of Jeshua during his time of his ministry, for Mark was only nine years old at the time of Jeshua's crucifixion, according to Paul's memories. The first of the Gospels was written by Mark around the time of Paul's death, in the year 65 A.D. Jeshua died somewhere around the year 33 A.D. So it becomes apparent that some 30 years or more had passed between the written word of biblical accounts and the actual events in Jeshua's life. For over 30 years, the story of Jeshua had been repeated over and over again, from one person to another, before being written down. That was the way information was preserved in those days — through an oral tradition. It was extremely expensive, as well as difficult, for people to write down information. Papyrus, or goat parchment, was required to write down a single copy of any document or letter. To make additional copies, a person would have to create them by hand, one at a time, using the same laborious method.

For over 30 years, the story of Jeshua had been repeated, before Mark put the story to parchment. It is his document that some biblical historians call the "Q Manuscript," the primary source of information for the other Gospels. Other biblical scholars assert Thomas was the author of the Q Manuscript and that Mark, as well as the other gospel writers, drew from the Q Manuscript[2]. Obviously, because of his young age, Mark received his information through hearing stories from the other disciples, who were grown men at the time Jeshua walked the earth. Mark, himself, was somewhere around the age of 39 when he decided to write down his version of Jeshua's life, most likely for a new generation.

As for the Gospel of Luke. As Paul tells us, unlike the other gospel writers, Luke was Greek, and did not know the Judaic faith nor the dominant language of that area of the Middle East: Aramaic. Luke had been a pagan — later to become a gentile Christian — who accepted Jeshua. Since Luke had never met Jeshua, never lived in Jerusalem, and most likely received all his information from the other apostles, or from repeated verbal stories, one has to ask to what degree of accuracy can we attribute toward the writings of Luke?

J: Thank you. In looking back over all that has happened since Jeshua's crucifixion, is there anything you wish you could have done differently, or that you wish you could change?

P: I wish that I could have had a greater influence and understanding. First of all, I wish I could have had greater understanding. I thought Jeshua was a threat to the Jewish leaders, to the Levites who managed the temples of the Sanhedrin. The Levites ran the temples. And I thought that's where the threat was, and would eventually cost Jeshua his life. I had anticipated that, and not the fact that he would become a threat to the Romans. So, I wish I had understood that better, and could have influenced him. Not that he would have accepted my thoughts, necessarily. He made his own decisions. But obviously, if he had been able to

---

2 *The Lost Gospel: The Book of Q & Christian Origins* by Burton L. Mack; Harper San Francisco, 1994

anticipate it, he could have backed off in some of the areas that caused concern, which cost Jeshua his life.

J: So you're really saying that the Romans were the real threat, not the Levites?

P: The Romans were the only ones who could take his life. There were no others. The Judaic laws were strictly civil laws. They didn't have the ability to take someone's life.

J: Why did the Romans feel Jeshua was a threat?

P: After Jeshua started doing his healings, he became very visible and well known in Jerusalem because of the miracles he was performing. And after Lazarus was revived — some say Lazarus had died, others say he was in a state of unconsciousness, but regardless, he was revived — Jeshua started drawing crowds in the thousands when he would come to speak and do healings. The Romans got frightened over the influence he was having — and they had no influence over him, as they did with the Sanhedrin.

J: They thought their authority could be undermined?

P: Yes. Here was an individual with whom they had no relationship, who now was becoming tremendously influential among the people of Jerusalem. And they were constantly concerned about potential uprisings. But as long as the people were under the control of the Sanhedrin, the priests, and the civil authorities, there was little concern. But they became greatly concerned when an individual would become popular outside of these areas where they had control.

Nick's memories as Paul, around the time of his death, tell us of a time when the Judaic people were rebelling against Rome. Later, General Titus, with 16,000 troops, would lay siege to Jerusalem. During the following years, the Romans would create havoc and slaughter in Jerusalem, killing thousands of rebellious citizens fighting for their independence. The magnificent temple of Solomon would be destroyed. Shortly thereafter, Emperor Nero would declare the Christian community responsible for the great fire that burned down a large portion of Rome's inner city. Nero would respond by tying Christians to stakes in his castle gardens, soaking them in oil, and turning them into human torches. The brutality of the Roman empire would be especially felt by the Jewish people who also practiced the newly found religion known as Christianity.

This was the atmosphere that existed at the time the four Gospels were written. Is there any wonder that the writers took care not to alienate the Romans, and, instead, implied that Jewish religious leaders were responsible for the death of Jeshua? In spite of the fact that it was only the Romans who had the ability to try a person for a capital crime, and declare the death penalty, the writers of the Gospels were careful to have it appear that the decision for taking Jeshua's life rested upon the Jewish leaders, as opposed to the Romans, who had total control in such decision-making. This was one of the most unfortunate acts in the history of religion. This caution not to alienate the Romans, for fear of further reprisal, would become the false foundation for 2,000 years of anti-Semitism throughout the world.

Julia was beginning to realize that there may be more to the overall picture of what happened after Paul's death besides the politics of that time. But how to get access to such information? At the end of Paul's life, Christianity did not yet exist as a religion. Consequences of decisions made by Paul would not be realized for another two or three centuries, in some cases. Certainly, the world wanted to know why Paul's spirit and soul had returned to our era. Perhaps there were reasons that had not been brought forth in previous regression sessions. On one previous occasion, Julia had explored an aspect of Paul's memory not previously attempted via the oversoul. If one can gain access to higher realms of consciousness, what some psychologists might refer to as the superconscious, then one has the ability to explore a greater pool of knowledge within the soul. But this isn't always possible, isn't always allowed. It must be to the soul's higher good that such explorations are attempted, while making sure outside influences are not allowed in. Once before, such access had been allowed, and, at that time, cautions were announced by Paul's oversoul. So, diligently, Julia decided to move Paul's memories into the realm of the oversoul. This would allow questions of both Paul and Nick to be asked simultaneously. It would allow access to unknown knowledge if Julia were allowed entrance to such consciousness. Thus began a quest that surprised not only Julia, but any who would later hear the transcriptions.

J: Thank you very much. Okay. Let us leave this period of time. Take a breath. Let's please now direct your attention to your oversoul, your spirit-mind. Just imagine yourself moving up. Moving higher and higher. Good. Thank you. Can you tell us what you see and feel at this moment?

P: I feel God's love, God's guidance. I feel the power of God. I feel strength, spiritual strength.

What follows is the unfolding of Paul/Nick's spirit-mind. Keep in mind that both the personalities of Nick and Paul can be accessed (as can other lifetimes), and are present, as knowledge from the past, present, and future combined. In such a state of consciousness, there is no line drawn between what we call the past and the future. Time does not exist as we know it. It is with a certain delicateness that Julia must tread this realm, for her own cultural predisposition for linearity simply will not apply. She is a visitor into the region of Spirit.

J: We would like to ask if you could speak on our behalf as to what Jeshua might wish to say to us at this time and this place.

P: Jeshua commends you for your courage, and for your taking on the responsibilities of the mission we are all doing — that you are doing with Nick. You are being guided by Spirit and protected by Spirit. And Spirit is grateful for your accepting these responsibilities.

J: Can you relate to us whether those who were called apostles are in body at this time?

P: There were so many more apostles than what you think of as apostles.

J: Just speak of the original twelve then.

P: There were not originally twelve.

J: How many were there?

P: There were 70. It was modeled after the Sanhedrin, except these did not have to be a father with a son in order to qualify. Some have been here and already passed over. Not because of God's intent, but because of how society functions. If some had not passed over, they would all be alive on earth now, yes.

J: All 70?

P: And many more that came after the 70, who also became teachers (*apostuli*). All, who were there 2,000 years, who played a part, a positive part in the messages of Jeshua — helping to provide that message to others — their spirit and souls have been born within this lifetime. All, except those who, for one reason or another, have already left their bodies because of accidents or wars or things of that nature, are now on this earth plane.

J: Is there a beginning date for what you're calling "this lifetime"?

P: They would, at least, be teenagers by now.

J: Teenagers or older?

P: At least teenagers. Some are as many as 80 years old, who have done things to pave the way, making it easier for what you are now doing.

To some, such information might come as a surprise, while others would point to references from spiritual adepts and noted seers of the past, such as Edgar Cayce, who had foretold the return of certain Apostles. Many letters, besides Kirk's, were arriving at the offices of the Great Tommorow referencing this great gathering. Hundreds of other letters came from people who adamantly believed they had been with Paul or the other Apostles when they had walked with the Master. But what to do about it now?

At first, efforts to ask individuals to verify their own past-life experiences, as Nick had done, proved what was even more important: that these individuals were having individual experiences. None has heard the calling for public exposure as had Nick. For their call was not the same as Nick's. Repeatedly, theirs was one of accomplishing that which they came here to help in: to prepare, support, and exemplify before the peoples of the world a new way of thinking, a new way of putting into action social concerns, social solutions, and spiritual ideals that would establish a greater world — a world based on peace, universal love and compassion, and a world not afraid to live in truth. Their letters, their e-mails and their phone calls left the impression that it is for them to tell their own stories their way. And so they shall.

12

ATIRA

*L*ittle Atira, you are so precious to me," Bessie continued. She watched as nurses passed by her hospital room. "You are my miracle child, just like your baby brother." Ricky had been born the year before, and his birth had blessed Bessie like a divine angel lifting the curse of barrenness placed upon her by modern medicine. "I will take care of you as if you are not mine, but God's. I have promised it so. You are a living miracle. Do you know that? Yes." She tickled little Atira's dimple, hoping her affection would not waken the peaceful child. She cooed, "Yes, you are my living miracle." Bessie was not a young mother but a woman close to leaving childbearing years. Though her face, surrounded by flaxen curls, did not betray her forty-three years, her innate wisdom did. Bessie understood how lucky she was to be able to have two infants, let alone one, who were medically unable to be here. Life had not been easy, but it also had not been rough. Richard, her husband, had provided well for the family with his work as an independent contractor and wall plasterer. But what he could not provide was hope for what now lay in her arms.

Five years later.

"Ricky," little Atira begged, "don't go down to the pond. And don't take that thing you're building ... that raft thing." Her older brother pretended not to listen. She wasn't supposed to be here but felt she had to follow Ricky and his neighbor friend who had sneaked away for their grand adventure. No one was supposed to go near the pond, for it belonged to a neighbor who bristled at anyone trespassing on his property.

Ricky looked up from his lashings. "What are you doing here? Go back home! Did Mom tell you to follow me?" For a six-year-old Ricky never did catch on well to the idea of limits or rules. His was a world of exploration. Tukwila was not like bustling Seattle just to the north. This area was still farmland and mini-ranches for the most part. Lots didn't hug up ten to a block. Neighbors did not hug either.

"No, Mom didn't tell me." She hesitated. "Dom did."

"Dom? That ghost friend of yours? Oh come on. You're just making that up. I s'pose he told you about the raft, too."

"Yes, he did," Atira began to pout. Ricky never believed in Dom, which hurt her feelings beyond description. For Dom was as real to Atira as Ricky. She never could quite understand why no one else could see him. He had first come to her in a dream not long ago, telling her he was her friend and would be with her throughout her life. To Atira, Dom looked about the same age as Ricky, except that Dom was very wise, seeming to know the answers to almost any question she had. "Dom said that you shouldn't take the raft into the water. He said there's going to be an accident and somebody's going to get hurt. Ricky, please don't go down to the pond!"

A small creek running down the family's property fed the pond. The cut of the ravine covered itself with a quilt of trees and bushes, perfect for young adventurers to sneak away and create unimaginable worlds. But this day, Ricky and his buddy, Tommy, had decided to be pirates. And pirates needed a ship as well as a sea — even if that sea belonged to someone else. He had been forbidden to cross onto Mr. Braden's property where the great sea's shore called to him and Tommy — who, after all, was a whole year older than

Ricky. "How'd you know about the raft, anyways? You been spying on us?"

"No. No, Dom told me. Please don't go to the pond. Dom says there'll be trouble."

"Oh, baloney," Ricky snorted while wrapping the last bit of twine around the gangly branches of his warship. "Go home. Leave us alone. And don't tell Mom or you're in for it. And take your Dom friend with you." Ricky could be so hurtful at times. Yet other times he was Atira's bestest brother in the whole wide world. Well — OK — he was her only brother in the whole wide world. Atira worshiped her older brother. However, she already had learned to trust the ways of her invisible friend. Dom's real name was Domsolis (Dom-saw-lis). Her three-year-old tongue had twisted awkwardly with the sound, "Dom Salts? Dom-all-us?" She eventually settled on "Dom." And the master soul, appearing in a child's form, seemed happy with that.

Atira pretended to head back home but instead hid behind a bend in the path. "C'mon, Tommy," ordered Ricky, "Let's go sail to an island and hunt for buried treasure. Do you have a sword?" Tommy stuck a broken branch, long ago bare of bark, into his belt as the two pirates began dragging their tethered assortment of branches and punk sapling trunks toward the pond. Some of the twine tangled in the brush, collecting twigs and sprigs, camouflaging the raft as if it were a walking bird nest instead of a potential sailing ship. Atira followed, spying how the boys struggled, dragging their craft to sea. And, deciding to be helpful, she skipped up to the raft as if she were meant to lend a helping hand. Ricky decided not to protest. As the children neared the pond, they noticed two other kids on the other side also seeking great adventure.

"You stay here," Ricky insisted to Atira as he clumsily pushed the two-boy raft into the water. Atira was not going to ignore Dom's warning. Statuesque, she stood silently with tiny hands twisted up against her mouth. What else could she do but watch? Tommy and Ricky shoved out to sea with poles in hand to guide their pirate ship. Triumphal whoops filled the air as the two pirates headed for deeper water. The pond changed to a great ocean as they poled until their poles no longer touched bottom. The deepest part of the pond stretched a little over eight feet deep, which meant the boys magically had to turn their poles into paddles as they drifted toward the middle.

Excited by their quest, Tommy stood up lifting his mighty sword from his belt, thrusting it skyward in true pirate fashion. "Crack!" snapped the the rotten sapling trunk under his feet. Startled, Tommy stumbled backwards, falling hard onto the flimsier part of the raft. More branches snapped as the raft began disassembling right before their eyes. Water surrounded Tommy's waist as Ricky tried to keep the twine from coming undone. With the main support of the raft breaking in two, the entire structure spread like flotsam. Tommy gasped for air as the great sea reached to his neck. Limbs and rotten log remnants refused to buoy him. Panic set in. Ricky, who'd already decided to swim to shore, realized his buddy could not swim. In fact, it dawned on him that Tommy was drowning. Alarm swelled in Ricky's chest as he pushed raft remnants out of the way, trying to reach Tommy. Finally, grabbing onto Tommy's shirt, Ricky hoisted Tommy upward as best he could, hoping his friend would find air. Tommy's flailing arms caught hold of his rescuer, latching on like talons, now dragging Ricky down. Both boys submerged, splashing like two birds in a birdbath — and then quiet.

"Oh, no," whimpered Atira, "Dom, what can I do?" Her little five-year-old arms grabbed the longest branch they could possibly carry. In near-comic awkwardness she struggled to reach her drowning brother and his friend with her little branch. Stretching as far as she could, the limb nowhere approached the twenty feet needed. Like a breaching whale, the combined bodies of Ricky and Tommy exploded on the surface, Ricky fighting to free himself from Tommy's lockhold. Dark confusion surrounded him as Ricky's mind thrashed at thoughts of escape or rescue. Wheezing for air, he tried one more time to force Tommy's head above water. Once again both disappeared below the spray.

"Dom, Dom, do something!" Atira screamed. She sensed the grave danger clutching at her brother. "Do something!" Across the pond, the two other boys bolted off at a run to find help. It would mean certain punishment, but all now realized peril stood near. Pirates and soldiers would certainly be punished when grown-ups found out what had happened. But something had to be done. "Dom," Atira shrieked, "you're bigger than me. Can't you do something? Please?" Tears trickled down her cherub face as her eyes ogled at her companion now walking across the water. Her mouth dropped open in awe, not realizing Dom could even do such a thing. She continued gaping as Dom approached the drowning boys, bent down and placed one hand on Tommy's head. The boy went limp. Immediately, Ricky turned the body around, forcing his buddy's head above the foam. Furiously he stroked the water, edging their bodies closer to shore.

Booming splashes erupted from behind Ricky. Strong arms grabbed him as two men pulled the friends apart, Ricky grabbing unconsciously, still trying to save Tommy. "It's OK, it's OK," a man's voice calmed. "I've gotcha. You're OK. You're OK." The two men carried the boys to shore, Tommy coughing up water, Ricky crying with relief. Atira gawked as Dom returned across the water back to shore.

"I didn't know you could walk on water!" she gasped as he eased next to her. Dom said nothing, Atira's awe interrupted by the realization she should check to see if Ricky was OK. Her little feet pattered around the shore until she reached the small crowd gathering around the boys. Mothers had made phone calls, and everyone but everyone in the neighborhood now knew of the incident. A kind of dread set in as Atira realized that Mom and Dad would shortly arrive.

As Bessie lectured her son on why mommies and daddies are to be obeyed, Richard held his daughter tightly in his arms. Pangs climbed from his gut to his heart as he realized how close he had come to losing his son. He set Atira on the dock as he listened to her chatter about how Dom had tried to help out. His hands brushed the roughness of the old pier as he wondered what words he could say to his son for his disobedience and to his daughter for her insistence on living in a make-believe world. "Daddy, Dom walked on water when he saved Tommy. I saw him walk on the water!" And before Richard could blink an eye, Atira took a step off the pier, her feet believing they could take footsteps as she plunged beneath the surface, with one hand reaching upward like a tiny Statue of Liberty.

Richard sprung to the end of the pier nearly falling in, himself, as his large hands instantly grabbed beneath the water searching for the first thing attached to his daughter. Panic ebbed as his hands clinched her dress, hoisting her out of the water like some giant crane. Suspending his drenched daughter midair, he barked, "What in the hell do you think you are doing? Are you crazy?"

Half choking from the bone-chilling water, half sputtering, unable to speak, little Atira began to sob. Through her sobs she squeaked, "Well, Dom walked on the water." Like a washwoman with a fresh load of wet laundry, Richard crushed his youngest against his chest.

"What am I going to do with you, you crazy child?" he murmured. "Don't you know that just because Dom does something it doesn't mean you can do it also?" It seemed like the right approach. Why scare her, why try and take her invisible friend away from her? She was a strange child with the dearest, sweetest heart in the whole world. He would do nothing to break her little heart.

"How did you know the accident would happen?" Ricky whispered insistently. Mom and Dad were couched in the living room discussing punishment for their insubordinate son.

"I already told you," Atira whined back. "Dom told me."

"You expect me to believe that?"

"It's true. Dom said there would be an accident if you went down to the pond."

"You mean it? He really does exist?"

"Of course he does. How many times do I have to tell you?"

The hushed tones in the living room rose to an audible level. Both children could hear the exasperation in their mom's voice. "What am I going to do? Do you know what she did last week? You were sound asleep at the time. She comes running into the bedroom like the house is on fire. 'Mom, Mom, come quick. There's angels in my bedroom. The angels are here. They're singing in my bedroom.' I mean, what am I supposed to do? So I go into her bedroom and there she is pointing them out. I ask how many are there, and she says, 'Oh, there's six.' And I ask, 'What are they wearing, child?' And she says, 'Oh Mom, they're wearing all this white glitter, like snow you spray on windows at Christmastime.' Snow spray? Where has she ever seen pictures of angels in snow spray? So I decide to ask for more detail. 'What are they doing?' And she gives me the funniest look — like I've lost my mind. 'Mom, they're standing in the corner over there, singing.' I tried to find out what was going on in her head. 'What are the angels singing?' She stands there as if she's listening to a conversation and says, 'They're singing to God about something, Mom. And it's really, really important.' I didn't know what to think. Ricky was sleeping soundly at the other end of the room, so I didn't want to carry on with her. But what am I supposed to do? I've talked to her about angels, told her to scoot over in bed to leave room for her angel to wrap its wings around her. So what can I say to her? That she's seeing things? They don't exist? Of course, I didn't tell her I didn't believe her. Instead I told her there's a reason why angels come. It's OK if the angels come to you. It's an important thing, and maybe something special just for you. I asked her if they were still there. She nodded her head but then got real quiet. Like she wasn't sure what the word 'special' honestly meant."

A sadness fell on little Atira's face as she remembered the night in question. A teasing smile snuck across her brother's face. "You saw angels?" Without saying a peep, she nodded her head slowly, remembering how disappointed she had been when Mom could not see the angels. Why had Mom talked about them if she couldn't see them? This had been such an exciting moment in her young life. The light had filled the entire room, and the song the angels sang had been so joyous. The discovery that Mom hadn't seen the angels was devastating to her; and worse yet, that Mom believed they hadn't really been there. Yes, she had been kind about not saying she didn't believe, but Atira was still devastated.

The voices dropped below eavesdropping range. "Bessie, I wouldn't worry about it too much. Don't you think this is something she is going to outgrow? Lots of kids have invisible friends."

"Not ones who seem to know what's going to happen before it happens. She's starting to have regular conversations with this thing, right out loud and everything, as if the whole bunch of us were having a tea party. When I asked her what she was doing down at the pond, she said that this Dom, or whatever his name is, told her there was going to be an accident. And when I checked with Ricky, he confessed that Atira had warned him to stay away from the pond. And then this walking off the end of the dock? What's she going to come up with next?" Bessie's Southern Baptist upbringing was scraping against the unexplainable events under her own roof.

"Yeah, her trying to walk on water was a bit bizarre. But I think she just has an active imagination. Nothing to fret about. She's such a gentle thing. Wouldn't hurt a fly. There aren't any kids in the neighborhood who play with her. If it weren't for Ricky, she'd be all alone."

"Richard. This is serious." Bessie pulled at the fabric of her dress, nervously wondering whether she should say any more. "She's starting to see little people. That's what she calls them: 'little people.' Just a couple of weeks ago she said to me, 'Mom, the little people say that if you don't put egg shells in this dirt here, the plant is going to get white blotches.' Egg shells? How does she make that up? I just smiled at her and told her the plant would be just fine. And the day before yesterday, I looked in my garden and noticed the plant had white blotches all over it. Egg shells? I mean, I don't want to encourage her, but I decided to crush up a few egg shells and mulch it around the plant ... just to see. You know." Her eyes checked to see if Richard's face disapproved of such tomfoolery.

"And?"

"And, well, the plant is looking better already." Richard's hand reached for his nose as if rubbing an itch, not wanting to let the turned-up corners of his mouth show.

"Little people, indeed. What's next?" she mumbled.

"Honey, this is like dolls, or the latest toy. She'll grow out of it. She's just like any other child who doesn't have neighbor friends to play with. When she goes to school she will change, she will outgrow it. She'll be interacting with other kids. Personally, I'm more concerned about that blanket she never lets go of. I think you're going to have a worse time getting her to school without that blanket than you are with her invisible friend."

Ricky poked his baby sister with his big toe. "How come you never told me about the angels?" Atira turned away. Her world was crashing down like melting snow off tree branches. *Why doesn't anyone believe me?* she cried to herself. With the determination of the family dog pulling on her favorite blanket, little Atira promised herself she would never talk about Dom again. Never. Ever, ever, ever. And for a five-year-old that meant about three months.

What is it about our society that we distrust anything out of the ordinary? Why do we try to label, torment, or demonize that which we do not understand? As Atira grew into her teens, her world grew more difficult. Either she would become a pariah because of her abilities or she would deny her giftedness for the attempted comfort of finding normalcy. She went for finding normalcy, to the point of telling Dom she would no longer talk to him. But normalcy would not be found. Before being diagnosed with dyslexia — not uncommon among the psychically gifted — she found herself labeled as stupid, slow, and difficult when in fact her mind perceived that which few others could, her wisdom enhanced by access to information that few find. Not until a psychic confronted her, almost insisting that she had abandoned her psychic gifts, did Atira move ever so slowly to a return to her gifts and her close relationship with Domsolis. In adulthood her reputation grew despite her hesitancy to take chances once again in a society that shuns what it cannot explain.

In Western Washington, with the pushing of her best friend Mary Ellen, known as "Angel Scribe" to her many readers on the Internet, Atira's renown reached the ears of Gary and eventually Nick Bunick. It was as though she were destined to play a significant role in the lives of both these men. After the release of *The Messengers*, Atira informed Gary that other apostles would seek him out. He had heard similar pronouncements from Sara who had said that the reincarnation of John the Apostle would find him. But Atira took that one step further. She became the instrument for finding these souls who had walked with the Master.

"Sweet Spirit," her voice bubbled with excitement over the phone one day. "I've met one of the other apostles. He's incredible. You've got to meet him. It's Bartholomew. His present-day name is Steve Koda. Honestly, I think you should give him a call." And that is how it all began. She would also discover the Apostle Philip at one of Nick's symposiums at Unity of Seattle. The man had traveled all the way from Missouri hoping that Nick would recognize him after the crowd dispersed. In spite of shaking hands with Nick and exchanging pleasantries, Nick had treated Michael Baumann no differently than any of the many who had attended. A bit disappointed, Baumann was about to leave when Atira corralled him, pulling him away from the crush around Nick.

"All right, who are you?" she asked point blank.

"Excuse me? What do you mean?"

Atira explained who she was and her connection to Nick. "I saw you from across the room. You had one of those giant rainbow angels following you. That usually means you were with Jeshua. So who are you?"

Michael stared at Atira for a few moments and decided to test her. He reached down into a pew nearby containing song books with biblical quotes, turned the pages, and handed the opened book to Atira. "I'm on this page," he offered, testing her abilities to make sure she was for real.

Atira looked at the page and instantly replied, "I knew it. You're Philip. You were with Jeshua. You came here to meet Nick, didn't you?" He confessed he had. "You have got to meet Gary. He's the one you should be talking to. Do you have an e-mail address or a phone number I can give him?" Baumann gave her his e-mail address, and then offered to take her out to lunch. Atira accepted, thus beginning a long and close friendship that would change the lives of Michael, Gary, and her. Because of what would unfold when the three would ultimately meet, a great adventure would be set in place. In fact, the adventure began when Atira later agreed that Steve Koda, Michael Baumann, Gary, and she should meet with Julia Ingram on Bainbridge Island, near Seattle, at Koda's home. All assented to participate in a combined past-life regression session with Julia Ingram. By this time Julia's fame as a therapist and author had spread because of the success of *The Messengers*. Atira wanted to find the reason why these past associates of Jeshua had returned at this time along with Nick, who had paved the way.

In the summer of 1998 all parties assembled among the thick cover of trees embracing Steve Koda's property. The smell of nearby Puget Sound provided an atmosphere of serenity and peace as the group sat to discuss how the combined past-life regression would work. Before arriving, Gary had changed his mind about doing a group regression and opted for all of them doing individual sessions if Julia felt she had the time and the energy for it. As was typically her way, Julia told the group she was there for them. Everyone agreed to go into private sessions without discussing with anyone else what they had experienced until all had been regressed. Since the last time Nick had suggested hypnosis with Julia, Gary was still apprehensive about allowing himself to be regressed, having had previous encounters under hypnosis that had left his life completely altered and difficult to explain. This session, as it turned out, would be no exception.

Steve, a patent attorney, escorted Julia to his home office, located in a section of the unattached garage where he worked on legal matters when he wasn't working at his office in town. After asking her if the room was quiet enough and comfortable enough for her to conduct the sessions, she smiled brightly with an "Of course. This will do fine." Gary and Atira chatted about why the various apostles were coming forward at this time. The only one who had not come forward as predicted was John. Like Sara, Atira insisted that John would find Gary. Be patient. Had not Steve and Michael B — as Gary liked to refer to him — found their way to this beautiful site?

After the sessions with Michael and Steve, Julia abandoned the confines of the dimmed office to stretch and to clear out the cobwebs with a short walk. On her return, she found Gary sitting in a deck chair on the patio, and with a smile said, "I think it's your turn." Gary was not looking forward to this moment. In fact, he had denied requests for any further regressions because of the increasing weirdness these sessions unloaded on his consciousness. After the initial encounter with the angel at Larry de Herrera's office, Gary had tried find out more information about the angel by going to different therapists. Each effort produced more visits by beings that could only be described as "otherworldly." The messages from these beings produced more anxiety than their appearances. Repeatedly, Gary was being asked to come out of hiding, to show the world the information being put at his feet. Like Atira, Gary had only wanted to be normal his entire life. And with events unfolding the way they were, normalcy was escaping him with increasing speed.

"Go ahead and make yourself comfortable," Julia cooed. "What is it you'd like to see happen in this session?"

"Well, I guess we should find out more information about my connection to the time of Jeshua. Everyone keeps asking me about that, and I keep not telling what I know because I'm not sure it can be verified, let alone understood." Previously, Gary and Julia had gotten into long discussions about the research she had explored and what she was finding out. The soul is a living mystery, and the information coming forward in her research and the research done by a fellow colleague, Michael Newton, PhD, was only beginning to lift the mask on the face of the New Psychology. While Julia had focused on exploring aspects of the soul in past-life regression, Newton had focused on information related to the soul before it entered the human body and after it left. Both were discovering that the soul is far more complex than previously thought. And events surrounding Gary seemed to confirm that.

As the session moved to the stage where Gary had moved into the subconscious, Julia decided to have him go to where he was guided. In the past, she had discovered that letting the client decide where to go while under hypnosis proved more beneficial to her clients than giving specific instructions. So rather than suggest he go back to the time of Jeshua, she simply asked him to explain where it was he had found himself. And much to her surprise, Gary was not in the past at all. He was in the future.

"OK, please tell me what it is you are seeing."

"I am seeing the Great Sphinx. There is a blinding light coming from the area that would seem to be where the heart of the Sphinx would be. The light is turning into an eye. It's talking to me. The Eye of Light is giving me instructions."

"And what is it telling you?" Julia asked.

"It is saying that what I am looking for will be found in the Heart of the Sphinx. 'Go to the Heart of the Sphinx,' it is saying. Now it is showing me what I will find when I go to the Heart of the Sphinx. There is a man dressed in a white galabaya, an Egyptian caftan, with a white cloth wrapped around the top of his head. He is one of the guardians of the ancient secrets. This man will tell me where we can find a tunnel that will lead to the Heart of the Sphinx."

"We?" Julia wanted to know if she had missed something.

"Yes, I can see three others who are with me. There is Atira to my left, Michael B to my right, and off in the distance is another man. I believe he is John, the one who has returned with John's soul. The Egyptian man in white is pointing to a tunnel. I can see where the tunnel leads. There is a room between the Sphinx and the Great Pyramid. There are objects in the room. I now see Baumann in the room. He is the one who will find this place."

"Can you describe the objects?"

"Some of them don't make any sense to me. There is one machine that holds these disks. On the disks is writing, which I don't understand. It's not hieroglyphics but like that. It's a symbolic language. When the disks spin they show information. There is another machine that holds an even larger disk. It is green in color. When it spins, things levitate. It is an antigravity device. There are other machines but I can't tell what they do. I am getting the sense, a message, that Baumann is to photograph this information and give it to a bearded man who will tell the meaning of the writings."

Julia tried to get as much detail as possible, and suggested that Gary would remember it all. When she tried to find how far in the future this event was to take place, Gary found himself standing in front of the Eye of Light again. The Eye spoke to him saying, "The path to the future is dependent upon the heart of man. Three hearts must come together as one for the path to be opened." And with that, Julia ended the session. After Gary had rested a bit and the two had discussed why he had been taken into the future, Julia suggested that Gary talk to Baumann. When he asked why, she simply replied, "Talk to Michael Baumann."

Atira was the last to go into the office for a regression session. While she took her turn, Gary sought out Michael Baumann and sat next to him. Michael wanted to know what had happened to Gary in his session. After Gary told Michael that he'd gone into the future, Michael wanted every detail. Upon giving all the detail, Michael stared at Gary for a while and finally stated, "I think you should know that I also went into the future. And to make this even weirder, I think you should know that I saw the same thing you did."

Upon hearing this, Gary's mind jumped back to the time when he and Nick had discussed going to Egypt to try and assist in uncovering the legendary Hall of Records. But the idea had born no fruit, and the topic never came up again until now. Was what he and Michael B had seen the Hall of Records? It didn't seem so, since the room was between the Sphinx and the Great Pyramid rather than under the paw of the Sphinx as prophesied by Edgar Cayce. So what had they seen? There really was only one way way to find out: Go to Egypt. But that is another story.

Atira, Angelic Mystic
Readings
(206) 767-5611
www.angelscribe.com/atira.html

13

THE ANGELIC PROPHECIES

W hen I ask Nick to recall his life two thousand years ago,"
Julia had said, "I am asking him to reach into a higher
dimension — to open his soul memory. He has an incredible ability
to do this with all of his senses, and with great detail.

"He is remembering a past incarnation of the soul that is
currently incarnated in another body, now known as Nick Bunick.
This we call 'soul memory.' When I ask Nick to reach into his spirit-
mind, I am asking him to move into that dimension to which his soul
has ascended. At that dimension, he is part of a collective spirit-
mind which is composed of more love, wisdom and intelligence
than one can imagine.

"This is where we go when we wish to access information
greater even than what previous lifetimes can reveal. This is where
prophecy happens, because spirit-mind — the oversoul — is aware
of the future."

Nick and Julia spent a great deal of care and consideration in
deciding whether to access his oversoul. Was it the right time?
Would it be permitted? Would it be the best way to inform the world
of what is to come? Nick had confessed that the angels had already

conveyed to him that it would now be all right to reveal what was coming to our planet — if it were done carefully and considerately. The only way to truly find out, was to venture into the realm of the oversoul. After asking about the apostles, Julia decided to edge closer to information relating to angelic prophecies that had been approached in *The Messengers*.

J: How do you understand what Jeshua meant by our "oneness with God"?

P: If you are not aware of God's presence in you, through his Spirit, then how can you be at one with something that you do not understand or are not aware of? What Jeshua tried to make people understand was their relationship with God, so they were aware that they are a part of God. To have total and fluent understanding is to become at one with God. That was part of Jeshua's spiritual goal.

If a person is born a great artist or a wonderful singer of songs, or a wonderful player of musical instruments, and yet has never picked up an instrument, or sung a song, or painted a picture, then they have no knowledge of these talents and gifts. So it is that Jeshua was trying to have people shed ignorance and have understanding of their relationship with God. He would try to use examples from their own lives to show how much they were missing if they did not understand or accept that they were a part of God.

J: What would Jeshua say to us now about oneness?

P: People have become polarized, and this is very unfortunate. They have been polarized through material means, based on the amount of wealth they have accumulated, or not accumulated. They have become polarized by their perceptions of geographic boundaries, by their political beliefs, and even in their religious beliefs. And this is wrong. They do not recognize that a much greater priority, a much greater value rests in the bonding that all people should have. We have one common Father and Mother, the Lord. We are all brothers and sisters. These barriers must be broken down.

J: Could you explain again what the 444 stands for?

P: It is as you have been told: the power of God's love. It has been used throughout history, although, many times, people have not recognized it.

J: Are there any instructions we can give to those who ask us for advice on how they can open to seeing their angels or hearing their angels?

P: For seeing the angels, visually, one must have spiritual sight into the other dimension. And that is something you cannot teach somebody. Nor can someone be taught to hear spiritual music or sound into that dimension. [Oftentimes, when the angels speak, it can sound like music being spoken, or chimes being made into words.] It is more important that they open themselves to their angels and spiritual guides through belief, meditation, and prayer.

J: Thank you. Some people's spiritual practices are based on the tenet that Jesus died for our sins, and through Jesus, we can be saved. Could you address this?

P: Why is it necessary to try to make people feel responsible for the death of Jeshua? These people are not responsible. Jeshua *lived* for us. He came onto earth as a gift from God. He had already reached perfection. But Jeshua did not have to come to earth again. He had completed his wheel, he had completed the cycle. So he came onto earth as a gift to us to show us the way, to be an example, and to offer himself as a conduit to God, to serve as our spiritual guide if we would choose to accept that offer. It has nothing to do with his death, or sins.

J: We would like to hear the reason why the soul and spirit of Paul has returned as Nick Bunick. Can you share with us why you have come back onto earth?

P: Yes. The first has to do with timing. In Nick's previous life on earth, he also had many of the skills and abilities he brings forth in this lifetime, now. But, it was decided to take his life when he was in his early twenties as a young soldier in France. The world was not ready, and it would not have been appropriate. The spiritual consciousness of the world was not ready to receive what he would have shared with them.

J: Was this during the war?

P: During the First World War is when his life was taken. Now he has been brought back at this time, as we approach the new millennium. There are many things he had to experience on earth to prepare him for what he is doing now. It would be through his experience in the business world that he would achieve the tools necessary before God sent him on his mission. Through the business experiences, he would acquire credibility to face the many challenges that are before him now. So it was a question of timing as to when his spirit and soul would be born again on Earth in a body, where he would be prepared to play a major role in the spiritual leadership in the world. As we approach the new millennium, this role will be made more apparent.

J: You said that God sent him on his mission. Can you tell us what that mission is?

P: One of the major responsibilities of Nick is to bring people together, to break down barriers. He is to bring together mainstream people of the world, regardless of their religious background or faith. He will bring these people together because he will be able to speak their language, and be able to provide understanding to these people that otherwise might not be heard. For there have been those who speak about God's laws who do not give credibility to those laws. They talk a different language. Do you want me to be more explicit? Do you understand what I am saying?

J: I understand. You speak of a new millennium. We have been told that there will be an ascension process occurring across the earth.

P: Why do you want to use words like "ascension"?

J: Please, if there is a better word, I would like to hear it.

P: Ideas are better expressed in sentences rather than catch-phrases. To select one word or phrase, such as you do in your political systems, causes adverse feelings, a lack of understanding or fear or, in some people, hostility. For instance, if one were to say to others, "I know a man who cares about feeding the hungry children of our world," hopefully people would applaud that man. But if someone said about the same man, "I know a man who's an extreme liberal," many that would have applauded him, instead, are turned off. It is nonproductive to create labels. It is better to speak of what is going to take place in sentences so people understand.

J: I agree. Can you give us a description of what will take place.

P: We speak of Earth, what is Earth? We are part of the Earth. Earth represents not only the physical planet, but everything that's on it including the vibrations of the Earth. Every physical piece of matter has an energy or vibration it gives off, even though we are not aware of it in most cases. People are the greatest example of giving off energy, which can be positive or negative, and in different intensities. We are going through a period of time when the frequency of the earth is changing, it is changing to a higher vibration — which in terms of energy means it will become less dense. And those who are in tune with the messages of universal love and compassion are also changing their frequency at the same time as the Earth is. Those who are not living their lives in truth, who do not have universal love in their hearts, who do not have compassion for those around them, are not changing in frequency. So they are being left behind. Again, it is as if we are going on a destination, and one is traveling in a wonderful automobile at a rapid rate of speed, and another is barely walking. If those walking have not reached a certain point on their journey by a certain date, they can no longer continue their journey in that environment. If they have not crossed that line by a certain time when the journey is over, if they have not reached that point on the mountain — which is not an unrealistic point — where they can see the top, then there will be a division with those on one side of the line continuing to live in this changing frequency, this new energy. Those on the other side of the line will live on a parallel earth, which will be at the lower frequency. These things are very confusing to most people who try to understand, so you must be careful how you share your words.

Indeed, in *The Messengers*, the angels had told Nick to keep this information quiet because they did not want people made to feel afraid. The angels spoke of a coming event, a rainbow of white light that would surround the Earth, which would be the signal event that these parallel Earths would be created through the arrival of a force of energy from the heavens. Those whose lives were based on universal love and compassion, those who chose to live their lives based on truth rather than fear would inherit a world of peace.

J: I hope that we can help as many people as possible to cross that line. Is there anything in particular we can say to help people?

P: You are doing it. It is not your responsibility to force them, to threaten them. The only thing you can do is educate them spiritually and make them aware of their spirituality. If they choose to reject what you have to offer, that is their choice, because God gave them free will to make that choice. You are helping in all you do.

J: It is my impression that one of our efforts is bringing back the original messages from 2,000 years ago. Is there additional material to be disseminated to people?

P: The soul is always evolving. What Nick has shared recently about the relationship between the soul and the spirit is valid. As the soul evolves, it continues on God's journey in a proper manner. It moves to a higher understanding of the spirit than it would have in previous incarnations. Although, at times, it can go the opposite direction, depending on experiences on earth. The messages you have today are not only those of 2,000 years ago but those that have been made contemporary based on what is going to happen in the future. They are, as well, based on understanding and relationships of the Spirit with God that has materialized and progressed over 2,000 years.

J: What is going to happen in the future?

P: After the new millennium has entered, there will be an alignment with the messages of universal love and compassion. Those that do live their lives in this alignment will bring unto Earth as it is in Heaven. The leadership of the world will become spiritually based, and, although there will be governments, people will look toward spiritual leadership for their guidance. I do not speak of religious leadership, although there may be some, who are religious leaders, who are able to make the transition into spiritual leadership. But it will be recognized that we will be living under the understanding of God's laws and of Jeshua's messages of love, compassion and truth.

J: Are there events that will be leading up to this new transition into the new millennium that we can speak of?

P: These events, as they happen, will become so obvious to everybody that they will speak for themselves. But if you tell them of the events before they happen, the focal point will come into controversy as to whether the events will happen or not. It is not in the best interest of your mission for people to focus on the events before they happen. Rather, understand these events as gifts that God is giving as signs.

J: Signs and wonders. I understand the logic of that. There have been a flurry of seminars and conferences where psychics were seeing earth changes, earthquakes, tidal waves and crazy weather. That's what people were talking about. They would ask, "Should I move from Idaho?" or "What about my mother in Florida?" The whole spiritual theme of the conferences was lost in discussions about real estate.

P: Yes. That's exactly what the concern is over, talking about events. It is better to understand that God's love is like sunshine. It is not in the shadows of fear that people should live, but rather in hope and anticipation of wonderful opportunities. There will be changes of the Earth, but not for punishment, and not for reasons of suffering, but because the Earth is changing its own vibrations and its own dimension. If a child believes there is a monster in the closet, to that child, the monster does exist. If a person believes that they are going to get into a driving accident, and drives with fear, it is only a matter of time until they will have an accident. People create their own darkness. People create their own fears. Those who live in fear create their own monsters. There is no supernatural evil force competing with God. It is that which each individual or group creates on their own that becomes their reality. If you live in sunlight, you do not fear darkness, for darkness is not a part of your life. If you choose to hide in darkness, then it is your reality and yours alone. There can be a collective darkness, just as there is a collective spiritual consciousness that is of the light.

J: Can you give us an idea of what the social fabric of the world will be like after this event occurs?

P: The responsibilities and changes will be many. We must concern ourselves about the children of the world. We have a great responsibility of taking care of the children. Likewise, we have a responsibility to the natural resources and the wealth of the world. For they must no longer fall into misuse, which has been happening for so long.

J: Do you see individuals or organizations addressing these needs?

P: Individuals will create organizations. Priorities will be so different because everybody will understand and be in tune to what the priorities are.

J: Will these organizations be based on an economic model or a community model or a business model?

P: All of the above. There will be tremendous challenges, which will take many forms. People who will have government positions will recognize that they will receive instructions from spiritual leaders. There will be tremendous cooperation among people throughout the world. Those who will remain on the new Earth will find uniform cooperation in determining goals and priorities with one another.

J: How will these spiritual leaders announce themselves?

P: They will not have to. They will be recognized. There will not be competition by ego or materialism. Their contributions will come from the heart. There will be no vainglory or seeking of position or influence.

J: Will there be nation-states still existing?

P: There will be nations because of the needs in different countries — culturally, geographically, as well as economically.

But there will be a spirit of cooperation throughout the world. Many of the barriers that exist today will no longer exist.

J: Can you give us an idea how this spiritual leadership will work?

P: There will be many different levels of leadership. But we will all be part of a team. Egos will not play a part in trying to hold a higher position of leadership. For some who have the skills, they will look after the children. To others who have the skills, they will look after natural resources. And to others who have the skills, they will formulate the education and training of people, as well as the training for spiritual leadership.

J: Thank you.

P: I must share with you again; if you make this a major issue, people will lose focus of what is happening, and, instead, will focus on events instead of what is important. You do not want that to happen.

J: You are trying to get across to us that everything is working just the way it is supposed to, and things are unfolding just as they ought, and we need to relax, not ask for details.

P: People's minds have been tainted for 2,000 years with false prophecies and distorted teachings. And as a result, they are programmed to think in terms of events being important rather than their own efforts in bringing Heaven and Earth together, as was the original intent. If people lose their focus on angelic events or miracles, then it will slow these events, even stopping them from becoming a reality. Do you understand what I am saying, or should I explain more?

J: If I were able to see the bigger picture ...

P: Let me say this. A person enters a university to receive an education, and all they can think about is receiving a degree four years from now. They become obsessed with reaching that day of graduation, which will result in receiving that four-year degree. So, instead, it ends up taking them eight years to receive the degree rather than the four years because their energies were focused on the obsession instead of the studying and learning.

One of the things that is unusual on this earth is the way people, in totally different degrees of spiritual understanding, are mixed together. It is as if you take children who are first-graders and second-graders, and mix them in the same classroom with college students who are juniors and seniors. They are all being educated simultaneously in the same classroom, in spite of their tremendous differences in awareness and capabilities. This creates chaos and confusion. And yet, that is the world you live in. You live in a world where political leaders, attorneys, managers of the justice system have a potpourri of people from different levels of spiritual understanding. You have people in positions of great power who are still in the second grade, spiritually. Yet others, who have great spiritual understanding, are given little or no positions of responsibility, because of the makeup of your society. This creates chaos and confusion. Do you understand what I'm sharing?

J: Yes I do. And in the Great Tomorrow, what would the classroom look like?

P: The focus will be on universal love and compassion, and living in truth — as opposed to the material world determining priorities and motivations for people. So it will be a totally different environment that will prevail around the world.

14

INTERVIEWS IN THE ANGELIC REALM

*T*hroughout history, prophets have existed in every culture known to man. It is only in modern times that the understanding of the purpose of a prophet is so misunderstood. For in modern times, the notion of prophet is synonymous with that of weather forecaster. Statistics on accuracy and clarity are issued forth with vivid computer graphics during the evening news. In the biblical sense, the purpose of a prophet has never been that of being a forecaster of events. Quite to the contrary, a prophet has truly fulfilled his or her purpose if and only if the prophet has changed the hearts and minds of people. In a way, the fulfillment of a prophet's prediction can be a testimonial of that prophet's failure. If the vision they foretell is one of calamity, such calamity can be avoided by human free will, changes of the heart. In other words, forewarned is forearmed. And if the calamity arrives, then the prophet has failed.

When Jonah proclaimed before the city of Nineveh, "In forty days shall Nineveh be destroyed," the people put on sackcloth and sat in ashes as a sign of their change of heart. For three days Jonah proclaimed that Nineveh would be destroyed. The king of that great city did not abandon its walls, seeking safety in a high-class condo complex in the mountains of Montana. Nor did he have Jonah beheaded in a attempt to stop the message by killing the messenger. Instead, this wise king pleaded with his people to change their ways, as he was about to. And on the appointed day of destruction, Nineveh still stood. Now, was Jonah proclaimed a false prophet and stoned to death? No. The people rejoiced over their ability to alter the forthcoming event with their own change of heart. What was true then is true now.

The admonitions from the oversoul of Nick and Paul are in complete harmony with the story of Nineveh. We have been instructed to look within for creating change, just as we are encouraged to find God-Within. Let no one minimize the power of Oneness with the Creator. Let us not look to the consequences of the future when plain truth dictates that what we do now is ultimately the determinate of what happens in our future. So like the people of Nineveh, let us study our hearts, and, if need be, change our ways — now.

But why do prophets also tell of us of forthcoming good events? Certainly, we do not wish to alter a coming blessing. There are two possibilities: One is to convey to people the reward for their goodness, and the other is to encourage people to embrace a single reality when two equally probable realities are coming — a kind of cosmic stacking of the deck. However, there is a risk in this. A man is told that he is going to inherit great wealth. So, he quits his job and waits for this wealth to come to him. But in quitting his job he finds out that the company is being bought out by a mega-corporation, and every employee stands to receive a bundle of money, for which he no longer is eligible.

If the vision given to society is one of great days and eras of peace, then humankind must celebrate the very source of such greatness so as to assure its arrival, as well as its blessing, thanking the very forces that will bring it forward. The purpose is to empower, reward, and assure a time of blessing warranted to a people deserving of it.

As Atira and others — who have access to the higher realms of conscious — will tell us, the angels say that human consciousness has changed so greatly in recent times, that even they cannot say with certainty what truly will befall the earth. All that can be pointed to are coming possibilities.

People have begged to hear what our world will look like after the coming together of Heaven and Earth. At presentations, Nick had been accused of elitism by not letting everyone know what a few were asked to keep quiet about. Now that Nick is able to describe for us what the angels have shown him, there comes an admonition with it: For those that have ears to hear, let them hear. Do not look outward for change. Do not become consumed with anxiety about events beyond you. For the only true way to change a family, a nation, or a world, is one person at a time. And that person is the one who is walking in your shoes.

In interviews with Atira Hatton and noted psychic, Laurie McQuary, who originally prompted Nick to come forth with his story, we find agreement: We are now in a time of great transition. "We may not have such a dramatic transition as it now appears," Atira hears from the angels, "because the level of awakening is so phenomenal at this time. The more people who awaken, the less painful, the less frightening, the less fearful the transition."

Laurie's prophetic attitude on this? "If I had thought the year 2000 was going to bring an end to the Earth as we know it, I would have gotten so depressed I would NOT have washed my kitchen floor. I would have cared less! You can't allow yourself to get out of balance with prophetic information." Especially when the purpose for revealing it is to bring us all back into balance. "Nick is right," she says with a kind of authority, "Get people away from this whole notion about physical changes. The real change that needs to occur is in the heart. I listened to him at a book signing. Even though I've talked with him many times, I wanted to hear what he had to say in public. And it really touched my heart to hear him talking about 'You know, I'm just the conduit.' And this is what I tell people about *The Messengers*, when they come in here all worked up about this coming of a new world. 'What does it really mean?!!' I keep getting asked. What it means is that it gives you permission to seek your own spirituality. That's exactly what it means. And what Nick was saying is that we are all accountable. Being accountable for our own spiritual state of being is what these coming events are all about.

Personally, I think many of these coming disaster kinds of things, whether it's El Niño or new viruses or whatever, can be changed with consciousness."

Both Atira and Laurie convey the same message: We can change our world by changing ourselves. And if we do not get the message in our hearts, then we get to see the message in our lives. "People end up learning to help and heal each other because of a disaster," says Laurie.

And Atira echoes this message. "You know, disasters are only disasters if you perceive them as that. People learn out of disasters. Unfortunately, we choose to learn through the physical manifestation when sometimes we could learn the same lesson by dealing with our own inner turmoil, our own inner disasters."

Others say we must heal one another if we are to heal our Earth. Those of us who choose greed, war, terrorism, hate, or deceit will inherit those very choices as our lesson-bringers. Some will not want to face their lessons now and will, instead, choose death. If enough of us heal our own hearts, if enough of us find our own inner balance with love, compassion, and truth, then we can act as healers for those in need of healing the negativities of their own lives. We can heal ourselves, we can heal people, we can heal society, we can heal our planet.

The transition period we are presently witnessing is providing us with just such options. Who of us does not feel we are dealing with our own personal turmoil like never before? Who of us is not seeing the need for our world to be healed? And who among us is not hoping that something can be done about it? Certainly there exist those who are blind to all this. But, by our own example, even they can be made to see.

"People think they're so separate from one another," says Atira, "so separate from their angels, so separate from God. It just isn't so. We forget we have a direct communication line at all three levels. I find that the more I ask for help from my angels, the more they become a part of my life, and the easier my life becomes, and the more aware I am of God's love, God's Spirit. We must recognize this inherent Oneness we have access to, because we think we're so separate. And if we remain in that separateness, we create fear and we create turmoil."

Both women agree that there will be changes in the structures of society, government, economics, and religion. "For some people, that's disastrous," says Atira, "while others will say 'It's about time.' " What most of us seem to forget is that peace is not the absence of tension. Nature proves that to us in the most beautiful of ways: the balance in a towering sequoia as its immense branches spread embracing the sky; the peaceful grandeur of the human body framed by muscles pulling in balance as muscle tone provides breathless grace in the glide of a ballet dancer or the dunk-shot of an athlete; natural bridges of rock suspending tensions across a divide filling the eye with wonder. From the wing of a bumblebee to the ambling of the great Colorado through the Grand Canyon, we see forces that could wrench into chaos in a moment's notice if not for the balance, the peace, the harmony of unfathomable forces.

While Laurie McQuary is explicit about events involving the period of transition, Atira presents us with a fascinating picture of a new Earth. In *The Messengers*, Laurie played a key role in the story, pushing Nick to meet with Julia Ingram, co-author of the book, which emerged from the past-life regression sessions with Nick Bunick. Since the first day Nick walked into her office, Laurie continued to function in a guiding role helping to unfold this incredible story. Laurie is a no-nonsense kind of person who "tells it like it is." If you don't like it, well, that's really your problem. She speaks just as honestly in portraying the transition period with which we presently find ourselves struggling.

"I've been saying for the last ten years — and I'll throw it out to you — what I've been telling other people in readings: I think the government as we know it is going to go. I think it needs to go. I don't think it's going to stop tomorrow, but I think we are going to continue to have real problems with the government cutting out, not supporting people. So people are going to start recognizing that what they needed to do all along was be responsible for themselves.

"I think we are looking at a time period of between the next three to six years," she declares with an even voice, "where health care is going to be different. Major changes will be starting. It's not going to be something everybody's going to be up in arms over, crying, 'Oh my God! We have to rebel!' I spent fourteen years in intensive-care nursing. One of the reasons I got out was because of the bureaucracy — not because of the patients, I loved the patients. So the health field is falling to its knees right now. And what you're going to see is more people in areas like physician-assistant programs, people who are going to be available because the hospitals, as we know them, aren't going to be able to sustain the present system.

"My gawd, twelve years ago, when I quit nursing and started this work permanently, I could not afford health insurance. And I only had one child then. I simply could not afford the insurance. It took me two years before I could afford the premiums. That situation is going to become a reality for everybody."

Others see the day when medicine will no longer be in the hands of doctors, but in the hands of healers. In discussions with other seers we hear, "In the future, we will lose faith in our healthcare system for the simple reason that it has been irresponsible, actually causing illness because of overprescribing of drugs, creating addictions for the same reason." Many hold the system accountable for what they call "the silent epidemic" caused by irresponsible use of antibiotics: pandemic candida (yeast) infections that weaken the body, superbacteria increasingly showing up in hospitals, imbalances in immune systems from a bureaucracy that rarely looks at the root cause.

Atira echoes the words of fellow clairvoyants: "Medicine and doctors are having to come off of 'God-status.' The healthcare system will have to face what it should have faced long ago — to be true healers."

Laurie and Atira see the day when healing centers will ultimately replace hospitals. "There will be many ways such healing teams will be made available to people," says Atira. "Many will discover the power in the God-That-Is, the Spirit-That-Moves-Through-All-Things. Whether it's homeopathy, massage therapy, Reiki, hypnotherapy, Chiropractic, medicine, or laying on of hands — whatever — everyone's personal injury experience or illness, disease — can be addressed by the needs of the person with the help of a team. People will also be helped by their connection with their angels, knowing that they're real. That is the area I think we need to look to the children for."

Many of these seers talk of the day when doctors will work not only with the body, but also the mind and the spirit as well. A wholistic approach to healing will not only be embraced, but so will a new mechanism of preventive intervention. Classes, workshops, instructions on how to keep oneself in balance so that disease will not even have a place to start, are already in the works in several areas of the country. It will take time for people to recognize this wholistic movement; however, the demise of our present healthcare system will only accelerate it.

"There will have to be healing centers," says Laurie in her matter-of-fact way. "These have been quietly talked about for a long time. You can't imagine how many people I've talked to, in the 26 years I've lived here, who have said, 'Oh, my dream is to have a center.' Well, it's going to be a dream come true, because we will *have* to have these centers. That's why naturopathic medicine is coming in so strongly. And obviously, we need to wed the different philosophies of medicine. If I have my appendix bursting, I don't think I want to go to a naturopath; I want to go to the hospital and have it taken out. *But*, prior to that, it could have been treated by a naturopath, never getting to the point of being poisonous. We're going to have health centers take over because I think the massive need is going to be so great."

Laurie and Atira go on to say how we are being blessed with a growing number of gifted people who have the capacity to heal in many different ways. Many people have incarnated at this time to help others through this transition, to help stabilize our changing way of life. Laurie sees healers, seers, and spiritual adepts eventually moving into their own communities where they can preserve the land, the attitudes, the natural forces required in bringing balance not only to the body, but also to the mind and spirit, and even the Earth.

Nick's oversoul revealed that five spiritual leaders will come forth to usher in a new kind of world. Three of these spiritual leaders will be men and two will be women. It is a topic that the angels increasingly share with him. These will not be religious leaders, for the notion of religion, as we know it, will continue to falter and wane. In describing their rise to prominence, Laurie says, "It's always been my experience, for all these years that I've worked with the other side, that time is very hard for them to give us. Time does not really exist on the other side. And in any readings, I always tell people, 'It feels like it could be a year or two, but ....' They have no time over there. I would see the emergence of these leaders as being down the line. I think that's something that's going to crop up here in the next three to five years. I think that's going to be after the really heavy-duty stuff has started to kick in. After all, that's usually what it takes for people to pay attention."

A bright smile beams across Atira's face as she describes the days when the five spiritual leaders are listened to by the planet. "By being totally awakened, they can be in many places at many times. They can use energy in different ways to the point of stopping conflicts, being able to address problems before they even manifest into reality. They will be like a high council, but not over any country. There will continue to be levels of government in each country, but not as we know it today. These government bodies will have far less influence than they do today. As an example: If they saw a rebel cause arising in Mexico, there would be a way of going there and resolving it before it becomes an issue manifesting as civil war, before arms are used and bullets fly. The need for arms, around the world, will diminish dramatically. The money spent on military armaments will be used for the betterment of humankind in peaceful ways."

Atira goes on to describe the kind of society that arises after the days of transition. "In every country there will be a middle class, an upper class, based not on how much income they bring in, but based upon their spiritual development. There will be people whose job it will be to keep peace and harmony, to monitor forces that are disruptive. To take care of these disruptive forces, there will be people who do healing work, on many different levels — healing individuals, animals, families, regional conflicts, and even the Earth herself.

"The five spiritual leaders will activate the various levels of what needs to be done in a given country. Each country will have corresponding centers or strata of spiritual purpose. All levels of conflict, whether personal or group-based will be addressed. After all, it is the collection of individuals with personal problems that tend to cause problems for the rest. So these gifted people will be able to be sent in and work with areas where problems are developing. Not wait until a war breaks out or conflict erupts. Those involved in disruptions will have to face the source of their own personal turmoil. We tend to hate anything outside ourselves that reflects our own personal flaws. So, it's at a personal level that people will be brought together, brought into healing."

What these clairvoyants are seeing is a world of peace. Not a Pollyanna world of hearts and flowers or rose-colored glasses, but a world where growth, resolve and turmoil are surrendered in a consciousness of healing, cooperation, and communal support. The five spiritual leaders will be the hub of this worldwide wheel of spiritual emphasis that turns on the path of universal love and compassion.

And how will these spiritual leaders command respect? We are told that it will be like walking into a room occupied by Mother Teresa or Gandhi — there's a reverence. Respect is automatic, for it will come from the heart. Only the most hardened of hearts would be able to ignore such loving entities, such compassionate souls.

Laurie takes us a step further into the detail around this upcoming world of spiritual consciousness. "There will be other Apostles here besides Nick. I don't believe they are all here in the United States. I think there are six more who are going to surface. One could be in South America. And I think ... hmmm ... one could come out of the British Isles. There are two here in the United States, and two more someplace in Central Europe. The problem is, I don't know if all these people are in tune with who they are. When these books go international, you will see some stuff surface. And, of course, what you don't want are the wannabes. They will have to be separated out. But I wouldn't worry too much about where these people are. Even if they don't consciously know it, they are here to do whatever work needs to be done, whether that affects whole communities or only ten people in their lives. They are here for the purpose of doing their work again."

But what about world religions? How will they react to these spiritual leaders as their influence grows?

Laurie's reaction to the question is immediate. "I think the role of religion has been addressed for the last several years. We're starting to see some real truth-telling going on. Eventually, people will fall away from religion, as we know it, and move toward a world-based belief system. The word 'religion' won't apply. It will be based on spirituality, not religion. People will finally come to recognize that we create our own world through what we think. You know, prejudices, bigotry — everything negative we've ever talked about for hundreds of years — is going to become a reality if we don't change that. We have to change our attitudes, our compartmentalized thinking. There's no leeway anymore. We have to start caring for each other physically, emotionally, and spiritually. I'm personally immersed in Native American spirituality. Which is merely love of the Earth — it's love of Nature. If people just did something like that — even if they still wanted to stay Presbyterian, it would be fine. But if we just honor where we live, *that* could become a world religion, a world belief system. Of course, isn't that what environmentalists are really talking to us about?"

The angels tell us that business and environment will no longer compete in this new world. Economies will no longer operate on supply and demand, survival of the fittest. Instead, economics will be based on supportive, cooperative models. "It won't be who can outdo whom," Atira says, quoting the angelic guides. Her eyes are constantly darting back and forth between invisible beings while the conversation goes on. "In the new business world, the real power will lie in the power of understanding one another, working with one another. There will be people who will be wealthy, but it won't be a selfish kind of wealth." Businesses will no longer focus on taking from the Earth, but how to nourish it. Atira tries to relay a message from the angels that can't be translated. "They are talking about a different form of recycling that we can't even fathom now. It's a regeneration of the Earth. The sparks of this are only now developing." Her eyes go wide as she sees a picture that defies her understanding.

Laurie reminds us of the world in which we dwell today. "What I frankly think is let's live in the here-and-now. What we do today is what we're going to create for tomorrow. I think we have some years to do something about this world we are going to inherit. I honestly believe we all have this incredible ability to connect with everything in the universe at any time. We've managed to cast everything into black and white. Our world does not operate in black in white, it operates in many colors. Yet everything has been narrowed down to probabilities. Everyone wants prove-ability, quantification on the physical plane when in actuality, what I think we still need to be looking at is the faith inside ourselves, trusting in ourselves — a spirituality that knows no bounds. No religion, no physical body, no limited thought." We are the makers of the days of wonder. Are we willing to believe that?

THE END

Laurie McQuary Readings
503-636-1832
www.lauriemcquary.com

Interviewed in the book
Psychic Criminology
by Whitney S. Hibbard
    Raymond W. Worring
    Richard Brennan

RESOURCES LIST

The Days of Wonder are about Oneness. It is in working together that we discover the power of our different gifts contributing to the whole. The following are people who foster Oneness and help others to do so:

Nick Bunick
The Great Tomorrow
P.O. Box 2222
Lake Oswego - OR 97035
www.TheGreatTomorrow.org

GW Hardin
DreamSpeaker Creations, Inc.
P.O. Box 16134
Missoula - MT 59808
www.gwhardin.com

Atira Angelic Mystic
P.O. Box 68207
Seattle - WA 98168
206-767-5611
www.AngelScribe.com

Mary Ellen "Angel Scribe"
P.O. Box 1004
Cottage Grove - OR. 97424
www.AngelScribe.com

Prayer Team
AngelScribe.com/prayteam.html

Laurie McQuary
Readings
503-636-1832
www.lauriemcquary.com

Michael Hoefler
Awakenings
P.O. Box 517
Victor - MT 59875
406-642-3630
awakenings1@qwest.net

Harvey Caine
Synergy: Fully Integrated Healthcare
1605 W. Garland, Spokane - WA 99025
509-245-3838.

Doreen Virtue
Inspirational author and lecturer
www.angeltherapy.com

Marianne Williamson
Inspirational author and lecturer
www.Marianne.com

Julia Ingram
Regression Therapist
Inspirational author and lecturer
2550 E. Ft. Lowell Rd.
Tucson - AZ 85716
Internet and Telephone Counseling:
520-319-6444
RegressionTX@aol.com
www.juliaingram.com

Joey Klein
Health and Wellness Center
P.O. Box 44
Andover - KS 67002
www.joeyklein.com

Association for Research and
Enlightenment, Inc.
A.R.E.
215 67th Street
Virigina Beach - VA 23451
800-333-4499
www.edgarcayce.org

Childhelp USA
480-922-8212
www.childhelpusa.org

Hay House Inc.
P.O. Box 5100
Carlsbad - CA 92018-5100
800-654-5126
www.hayhouse.com